Midget Ninja
and Tactical
Laxatives

Midget Ninja and Tactical Laxatives

Philip Sidnell

Pen & Sword
MILITARY

First published in Great Britain in 2012 by
PEN & SWORD MILITARY
An imprint of
Pen & Sword Books Ltd
47 Church Street
Barnsley
South Yorkshire
S70 2AS

Copyright © Philip Sidnell

ISBN 978-1-84884-331-8

Typeset by Concept, Huddersfield, West Yorkshire.
Printed and bound in England by CPI Group (UK) Ltd, Croydon, CR0 4YY.

Pen & Sword Books Ltd incorporates the imprints of Pen & Sword Aviation,
Pen & Sword Family History, Pen & Sword Maritime, Pen & Sword Military,
Pen & Sword Discovery, Wharncliffe Local History, Wharncliffe True Crime,
Wharncliffe Transport, Pen & Sword Select, Pen & Sword Military Classics,
Leo Cooper, The Praetorian Press, Remember When, Seaforth Publishing and
Frontline Publishing.

For a complete list of Pen & Sword titles please contact
PEN & SWORD BOOKS LIMITED
47 Church Street, Barnsley, South Yorkshire, S70 2AS, England
E-mail: enquiries@pen-and-sword.co.uk
Website: www.pen-and-sword.co.uk

Contents

To my oh-so-patient wife Kerry and my two cheeky monkeys,
Alexander and Emma

and I wonder
when I sing along with you
if everything could ever feel this real forever
if anything could ever be this good again

Acknowledgements

I must start by thanking my boss, Charles Hewitt, for letting me write this book and everyone else at Pen & Sword who has contributed to the finished article – especially Paula Hurst and Matt Jones for chasing me along and Jon Wilkinson for the jacket design. Thanks in advance to the Marketing and Sales posse – when you've sold enough copies to make me rich I'll buy you all a drink.

My gratitude is also due to all those of my fellow authors who answered my call for their favourite military curiosities (some of you revealing a very strange sense of humour in the process), provided me with details or helped me with pinning half-remembered snippets down to actual sources. If I don't appear to have made use of your particular contribution, that doesn't mean your trouble was unappreciated (and there's always volume 2). Dave the Bear, thanks for general encouragement and also for the tip on the lizard thing; still can't believe that turned out to be true. A special mention in dispatches goes to James Cole who spent a fair portion of his work experience placement helping me with my research. My former colleague and friend, Andrew McClellan read the first proof and gave some very constructive criticism just in time, so sincere thanks go to him.

Of course, I will never hear the end of it if I don't reserve the biggest thankyou for my wife and children. Even if you did often get in the way of actually writing the thing you are always an inspiration; besides, I can't imagine a more wonderful trio of distractions. Thanks for making life so much fun.

Introduction

I became fascinated with all things military when I was just a small boy but, unlike many, I never grew out of it. In recent years I have been fortunate enough to make a living out of military history as a book editor, so warfare occupies my thoughts for a large proportion of my waking life. The word 'geek' has been used on more than one occasion. I know family and friends sometimes find this preoccupation with man's efforts to kill or conquer his fellow man a little morbid. I suppose it could get a little grim or 'heavy', if it wasn't for the fact that the annals of human conflict are liberally scattered with plenty of lighter moments; quirky characters, bizarre incidents and tragi-comic mishaps that make me shake my head in wonder as I read, giggle or even laugh out loud. It is surprising how often I relate these bits to those same family and friends who find my interests odd or who are just 'not into' military history, only to find they, too, are amused or amazed. This book is basically a collection of some of those bits.

Collectively, the assembled material displays the best and the worst of the human condition. There are tales of inventive genius, endurance against the odds, honour and nobility of spirit; but there is also despicable deviousness and deceit, hapless blundering and the sort of harebrained lunacy that would make Wile E Coyote look like a paragon of caution and common sense. I hope you enjoy reading this as much as I enjoyed writing it.

Philip Sidnell
Teynham,
September 2012

p.s. If your favourite strange stratagem or weird weapon is not in here, why not contact me via the Pen and Sword website and share it with me? (www.pen-and-sword.co.uk) Maybe I'll put it in a future volume.

Chapter 1

War Elephants and How to Beat Them

Where did you get that Elephant?

At some point around 4,000 years ago, if not earlier, some brave (or crazy, or drunk or all three) fellows decided it would be a good idea to climb onto the backs of some elephants and teach them to obey their commands. We can't be sure how much time passed between first domestication and the day these first elephant riders hit on the fun idea of using their new toys against their enemies. But, human nature being what it is, we can bet it wasn't long.[1] War elephants remained in service as front line warriors up to the eighteenth century AD and even later as military transport and engineers.

The elephant's military potential seems obvious. They are very big and very scary, highly mobile (they can outrun a human over short distances) and armed with tusks to gore and a trunk to grab or swat the enemy. In most armies their natural armament was augmented by placing a crew of several warriors on their backs, usually in a turret or howdah, armed with an array of weapons such as bows, javelins and pikes, and later even with muskets or small cannon. Often, particularly in Indian armies, the elephants themselves could be armed with huge swords, maces or chains gripped in, or attached to, their trunks. While their thick skin and sheer bulk meant they were very hard to kill with primitive pre-gunpowder weapons, they were often given the additional protection of armour.

Elephants could even be used to batter down fortifications. In some cases they butted or leant on gates or palisades with their foreheads, much as they would push over trees in the wild. But on at least one occasion elephants were actually used to wield battering rams. In AD 1001, when Sultan Mahmud, the first Ghaznavid ruler

1

of Eastern Iran wanted to attack Taq (also known as 'the virgin fortress' because it had never been penetrated), he 'invented special devices' and employed 'five elephants fitted with rams and battering equipment for use against walls and buildings'. These 'attacked the gates of the fort, which crashed down under the furious charge of the elephants'. The defenders fought bravely at first but when Khalaf, their commander 'saw Mahmud's elephants trampling his men to death he offered submission and surrendered the fort'.[2]

Mind you, on other occasions, the elephant's size could make it a liability in an urban environment. In 272 BC, Pyrrhus of Epirus used twenty-four elephants in an attack on Argos (the Greek city that is – he wasn't taking them back to the catalogue store for a refund). The plan was to sneak a force that included some of the elephants into the city at night, when one of the gates would be opened by traitors within. The plan was going fine (elephants are surprisingly good at sneaking as their soft soles allow them to tread silently), until the elephants proved too big to fit through the city gates with their howdahs on. By the time the crews had removed the little towers and squeezed their mammoth mounts through, it was broad daylight and the city's defenders had been woken by the commotion. When, after some very confused street fighting, Pyrrhus attempted to withdraw his forces, another elephant coming up with the reserve had got itself stuck in the gateway and blocked their escape. This led indirectly to Pyrrhus' death. In 81 BC, without the excuse of darkness and an unfamiliar city, Pompey the Great's plans for a triumphal entry into Rome hit a similar technical hitch when the gates proved too narrow for his chariot pulled by four elephants abreast.

In open battle elephants could be devastating. It is hard to imagine the kind of fear felt by infantry facing a charge by a line of elephants; cavalry horses, unless specially inured to the experience, were sometimes panicked by the merest whiff of them. Even the vaunted Roman infantry was not immune to elephant shock as Plutarch's description of the Battle of Asculum (279 BC) makes clear:

> The factor which did most to enable the Greeks to prevail was the weight and fury of the elephants' charge. Against this even the Romans' courage was of little avail: they felt as they might

have done before the onrush of a tidal wave or the shock of an earthquake, that it was better to give way than to stand their ground for no purpose.   [Plutarch, *Pyrrhus*, 21]

But they did not rely entirely on psychological impact, the danger they posed was very real. The ancient sources are liberally sprinkled with vivid accounts of the devastating physical effect of elephants in combat. Here is a fairly typical one:

The elephants being made use of (by the mighty bulk of their bodies and their great strength), bore down and trod under foot many of the Macedonians; others were caught up in their trunks, and tossed into the air, and then fell down again with great violence upon the earth, and so miserably perished; many likewise were so rent and torn with their teeth, that they died forthwith.   [Diodorus Siculus, *Universal History*, xvii, 10]

No wonder that they are often seen as the tanks of the ancient world. Unfortunately for their owners, what happened later in that same battle was also all too common. Diodorus goes on to explain that many of the elephants:

ceased altogether to play their expected part, and, maddened by pain and fear, set indiscriminately upon friend and foe, thrusting, trampling and spreading death before them. [The Indians] jammed up close among them ... found them a more dangerous enemy even than the Macedonians.

Who ever heard of a tank that would suddenly run out of control and attack its own side? Even if the unpredictable pachyderms did not actually attack their own side, their morale was fragile. If one or two decided to switch to flight mode, the herd instinct might kick in and the whole lot could suddenly turn tail and stampede back the way they had come, trampling a path of destruction through any of their own side coming up in support.

An enraged or panicked elephant was so dangerous and so resistant to all reasonable requests from its mahout (driver) that a drastic forerunner of the emergency stop button was adopted in the form of a hammer and chisel. The Roman historian Livy, in his description of the Battle of the Metaurus River (207 BC), gives the credit for this innovation to the Carthaginian commander, Hasdrubal (brother of the famous Hannibal), but writes as though it later became general practice.

> More of the elephants were killed by their own riders than by the enemy. The riders used to carry a mallet and a carpenter's chisel and when one of the creatures began to run amuck and attack its own people, the keeper would put the chisel between its ears at the junction of head and neck and drive it in with a heavy blow. It was the quickest way that had been found to kill an animal of such size once it was out of control; and it was Hasdrubal who first introduced it.   [Livy, 27.49]

And if trying to control a herd of 5-ton, sword or chain-wielding pyschopathic beasts was not scary and unpredictable enough, why not get them drunk too? Apparently Indian mahouts thought their mounts just weren't dangerous enough sober and gave them wine to drink before battle. Whether or not the mahouts had to stop off on the way home from battle to buy them giant-sized kebabs is not recorded.

Perhaps it was because they were drinking buddies as well as colleagues that some elephants formed incredibly close bonds with their mahouts. This too could sometimes prove to be a liability. As Pyrrhus' forces tried to escape back out of the city of Argos, which they had finally managed to get into, one of his elephants realized that its driver had gone missing amid the chaotic street fighting and, perhaps trumpeting the drunken elephant equivalent of 'I really love you man', went back for him, as Plutarch describes:

> Another elephant named Nicon, one of those which had advanced further into the city, was trying to find its rider who had been wounded and fallen off its back, and was battling against the tide of fugitives who were trying to escape. The beast crushed friend and foe together indiscriminately until, having found its master's dead body, it lifted the corpse with its trunk, laid it across its tusks, and wheeling round in a frenzy of grief, turned back, trampling and killing all who stood in its path.   [Plutarch, *Pyrrhus*, 33]

Plutarch also recounts the touching behaviour of King Porus' elephant during his defeat by Alexander the Great at the Battle of the Hydaspes. Porus, incidentally, was said to be so big that when riding an elephant he looked like an ordinary man riding a horse.

> His elephant too was very large and showed an extraordinary intelligence and concern for the king's person. So long as Porus was fighting strongly, it would valiantly defend him and beat off his attackers, but as soon as it recognized that its master was growing weak from the thrusts and missiles that had wounded him, it knelt quietly on the ground for fear that he might fall off, and with its trunk took hold of each spear and drew it out of his body.   [Plutarch, *Alexander*, 60]

Porus was then easily captured. Another account of the battle (that of Quintus Curtius Rufus) states that when Porus' elephant knelt down, the other remaining elephants, which had been giving Alexander's men the toughest fight they ever faced, all followed its example and so ended their resistance.

Despite being something of a double-edged sword, their battle-winning potential was so valued that various armies across a couple of millennia went to great lengths to gather, train, feed and move forces of elephants over great distances. Here are some examples:

An elephant, an elephant, my kingdom for an elephant
In 304 BC, Seleucus I made a treaty with the Indian empire-builder Chandragupta Maurya in which he swapped a large swathe of territory, essentially the areas comprising modern Pakistan and Afghanistan, for 500 elephants and their mahouts. To sweeten the deal, he also threw in one of his daughters.

Ptolemaic Egypt – Keeping up with the Seleucids
Once the Seleucids had a fleet of elephants, their great rivals in Egypt, the Ptolemaic dynasty, just had to have some. Blocked from access to Indian elephants by the Seleucid empire, Ptolemy I started sending expeditions southwards into what is now Sudan, Ethiopia and Somalia to capture wild elephants for training. His son

Ptolemy II Philadelphus*, who came to power in 283 BC, founded a city called Ptolemais Theron (Ptolemais of the Hunts) on the Red Sea coast as a base for catching elephants. Apparently one of the methods elephant hunters in this region used to get close their targets involved smearing themselves in elephant dung to disguise their scent.

From Ptolemais Theron they were shipped to ports further along the coast then trekked overland to the Nile, where they could again board boats downriver to the city of Memphis in lower (northern) Egypt. As the elephant population dwindled through over-hunting, later Ptolemies had to establish ports further and further south. These ports had to have specially designed facilities, and even a special kind of ship was invented, to handle this precious living cargo. All this was a vast investment and the weapon system they were getting wasn't even the top-of-the-range Indian elephant. When Ptolemy IV's army faced the Seleucids at the Battle of Raphia in 217 BC, he had 73 African elephants to oppose the enemy's 102 Indian elephants. The Egyptian animals were not only outnumbered but individually inferior:

> A few of Ptolemy's elephants ventured to close with those of the enemy, and now the men in the towers and on the backs of the beasts made a gallant fight of it. ... Now most of Ptolemy's elephants were afraid to join battle, as is the habit of African elephants; for unable to stand the smell and the trumpeting of the Indian elephants, and terrified, I suppose, also by their great size and strength, they immediately run away from them before they get near them. This is what happened on the present occasion. [Polybius, *The Histories*, V.84.2–6]

---

*The Ptolemaic dynasty were not very inventive with first names, all the kings being named Ptolemy. Fortunately they all took on sobriquets, such as Ptolemy I Soter (the wise) or Ptolemy II Philadelphus ('lover of man' or 'benefactor') which helps make individuals more memorable. By the time the famous Cleopatra, the last of the Ptolemaic line, came to the throne, she was Cleopatra VII and at first shared power with Ptolemy XIII, who was both her brother and her husband, then with her younger brother named – can you guess? – Ptolemy XIV, whom she poisoned to become sole ruler.

Now wait a minute, I hear you cry. African elephants are bigger than Indian elephants, right? Well, the African Elephant (*Loxidonta africana*) is considerably larger than the Indian Elephant (*Elephas maximus*) but it is also untameable. A lot of people don't realize there are actually three species of elephant. The Ptolemies (and later the famous Hannibal) were apparently using the smaller African Forest Elephant (*Loxidonta cyclotis*), at one time thought to be extinct but found to be still living (if hardly flourishing) in central Africa and recently recognized as a separate species, rather than a mere sub-species. While not quite a match for Indian elephants, the African version was still quite big and mean enough for terrifying and stomping on enemy infantry and cavalry and clearly still warranted extreme logistical efforts to get them where they were needed.

Hannibal's elephant rafts and Alpine staircase

The most famous user of war elephants was undoubtedly the great Carthaginian military genius Hannibal. If Joe Public knows one thing about Hannibal it is that he marched an army of elephants from Spain to Italy via the Alps and thereby scared the bejabers out of the Romans. When Hannibal left Spain his army consisted of about 50,000 infantry, 9,000 cavalry and just 37 elephants, not that large a force by ancient standards. Coming to the Rhone, he found that the beasts, though they usually love water and are strong swimmers, were afraid to enter the rapidly rushing river. So he had several, large and sturdy rafts constructed, the first pair moored to the river bank, another pair lashed to them and so on until they formed a jetty about 50 feet wide and projecting some 200 feet out into the river. These were then covered with earth 'until they had raised its surface to the same level as the bank, and made it look like the path on the land which led down to the crossing' [Polybius III.46]. The elephants were now led along this floating path, two old matriarchs in the lead, until they were all standing on the last section. This was then cut adrift and towed by boats to the far shore. A few elephants panicked and ended up in the water but, although their mahouts were drowned, the animals themselves remembered they could swim or walked across using their trunks as snorkels (as they do in the wild).

This was not the only incidence of improvised elephant rafts. Frontinus [*Stratagems*, I.vii.2] records how the Roman consul Lucius

Caecilius Metellus, made rafts from large earthenware jars with planking over the top and ferried his elephants upon them right across the Strait of Messina that lies between Sicily and the Italian mainland. A distance of between 2 and 3 miles.

The next obstacle for Hannibal was the Alps. Although, as Polybius points out, Hannibal was neither the first nor the last to lead armies through the Alpine passes, indeed it was a veritable highway for invading Celts and Roman armies, the Carthaginian genius may have got a bit lost, was attacked by hostile tribes and experienced unseasonably severe weather with heavy snowfall. At one point his cold, hungry and tired army came to a spot where the path had been carried away by a landslide, leaving an almost sheer drop. The Roman historian Livy describes Hannibal's remarkable solution.

> The next task was to construct some sort of passable track down the precipice, for by no other route could the army proceed. It was necessary to cut through rock, a problem they solved by the ingenious application of heat and moisture; large trees were felled and lopped, and a huge pile of timber erected; this, with the opportune help of a strong wind, was set on fire, and when the rock was sufficiently heated the men's rations of sour wine were flung upon it, to render it friable. They then got to work with picks on the heated rock and opened a sort of zigzag track, to minimize the steepness of the descent, and were able, in consequence, to get the pack animals and even the elephants, down it. [Livy, xxi, 37]

By such Herculean efforts, Hannibal's elephants finally made it down into the north Italian plain in late 218 BC. Though he had lost about half of the rest of his army *en route*, none of the sources mention any of the elephants being lost. However, much of this effort was largely wasted. Hannibal did get to make good use of them in his first major battle in Italy, at the Trebbia, but all of them except one then promptly died from the effects of wounds, fatigue, malnourishment and cold. The sole survivor, Suras (the 'Syrian'), became Hannibal's personal mount, but the rest of his sixteen-year rampage round Italy was conducted without the benefit of an elephant force.

Elephant tobogganing

In 168 BC, the Roman consul Marcus Philippus was trying to invade mountainous Macedonia with an army which included twelve elephants supplied by the allied African prince, Masinissa. Finding all the passes fiercely defended by Macedonian troops, and rapidly running out of supplies, the consul hit on a daring plan. He decided to take a portion of his force on a wide flanking movement over the mountains, using little-used goat tracks. Surprisingly, he included the elephants among this select force and set off up into the mountains.

Soon the Romans were faced with a very steep, loose slope that they had to descend and the elephants began to panic and cause mayhem, particularly throwing the cavalry horses into confusion. Necessity being the mother of invention, Marcus Philippus came up with a plan. Large posts (presumably hewn from convenient tree trunks) were driven in a little way down the slope, a little further apart than an elephant's width. Timbers were laid across these and then earth heaped up against it until it formed a sort of ramp or platform projecting out from the valley side. This was repeated at intervals directly below further down the slope. The elephants were then led in turn out to the end of the first ramp, happy with the solid earth beneath their feet. The first pair of supporting posts were then cut away, allowing the earth to avalanche down, taking the no-doubt indignant elephants with it. According to Livy, some slid down on their feet, others on their backsides. The process was repeated at the next stage down until they had all reached the bottom. Most of the infantry apparently went down roly-poly.

The whole madcap enterprise succeeded. The Macedonian king, Perseus, was taken completely by surprise. As soon as he learnt some Romans were over the mountains, he assumed a major army had forced one of the vital passes, panicked and abandoned all the passes, which the Romans then occupied unopposed.

Elephant and castle

One war elephant may even have made it all the way to Britain, then considered the ends of the earth. In his book of stratagems, Poly-aenus credits Julius Caesar with taking a single elephant with him on his second invasion of that fair island in 54 BC. His first invasion had actually been a failure, resulting in ignominious withdrawal (though Caesar, our main written source for the events presents it otherwise), so perhaps Caesar was looking for a secret weapon to give him the edge. Polyaenus describes the disproportionate effect the elephant had on an enemy who had never seen anything like it.

> When Caesar's passage over a large river in Britain was disputed by the British king Cassivellaunus, at the head of a strong body of cavalry and a great number of chariots, he ordered an elephant, an animal till then unknown to the Britons, to enter the river first, mailed in scales of iron, with a tower on its back, on which archers and slingers were stationed. If the Britons were terrified at so extraordinary a spectacle, what shall I say of their horses? Amongst the Greeks, the horses fly at the sight of an unarmed elephant; but armoured, and with a tower on its back, from which missiles and stones are continually hurled, it is a sight too formidable to be borne. The Britons accordingly with their cavalry and chariots abandoned themselves to flight, leaving the Romans to pass the river unmolested, after the enemy had been routed by the appearance of a single beast.
>
> [Polyaenus, *Stratagems*, viii, 23.5]

This account is often discredited and there are some reasons for scepticism. Julius Caesar's own account of the invasion and the crossing of the Thames, which must be the river in question, makes no mention of an elephant and he isn't known to have used them in any of his other campaigns. However, it has been argued that Caesar, being the arch self-propagandist, decided there wasn't much glory in the enemy running away at first sight, rather than being out-manoeuvred and defeated in an opposed crossing and so omitted the elephant. Caesar did later issue a coin showing an elephant trampling a dragon, the symbol of Britain. And is it just coincidence that the nexus of roads leading to all the major Thames bridges from the south is still called Elephant and Castle? The name can only be firmly traced back as far as 1765 when an inn of that name is mentioned there. Although other explanations have been put forward, it is far from impossible that the name chosen for the inn reflected a surviving folk memory of the incident. Otherwise it is a remarkable coincidence.

Last flight of the war elephant – Operation Barrooom

One of the last military uses of elephants, though in a logistical rather than combat role, came during the Vietnam War. Teams of Green Berets of the US Special Forces were tasked with recruiting and training fighters from those mountain tribes opposed to the Communist insurgents. These Montagnards, as they were collectively known, were to be housed in training camps constructed in the jungle. Incredibly, cut timber to build these camps was initially flown in from the USA until some genius realized the jungle was full of trees and that trees are made from wood. So the Green Berets and Montagnards began cutting and hauling local timber using trucks and tracked vehicles, but the difficult terrain wore these out at a remarkable rate. Finally someone hit on the idea of using elephants, which were still used in this traditional manner in other parts of the country.

Captain John S. Gantt was tasked with acquiring suitable animals and he eventually managed to purchase two, the only trouble being that they were 365 miles of mountain and jungle away. It was decided the elephants would have to be sedated and moved by air. Initially the plan was to drop them out of the back of a C-130 cargo plane on parachutes but when the specialist sedatives required were purchased in Britain, the Royal Society for the Prevention of Cruelty to Animals got wind of the plan and made a fuss. To avoid any negative press the plan was changed. On 4 April 1968 the elephants were drugged and loaded onto the C-130 for the flight to Da Nang. From the airfield at Da Nang the elephants travelled the last 65 miles slung in cargo nets beneath a pair of helicopters. Safely back on terra firma they were given an antidote to the sedative and ridden off to their new quarters. Representatives of the world's press were there, looking for a feel-good story from the war zone for a change, but it was somewhat overshadowed by the assassination of Martin Luther King Jr the next day. Still, Operation Barrooom got its moment of glory nearly three decades later when Disney made a film based upon it, released in 1995 as *Operation Dumbo Drop* – not one of their best remembered films. But it was during the C-130 flight that the operation gained the unofficial codename by which its participants remember it – Operation Barrooom; inspired by the sound of one of the slumbering beasts farting within the confines of the cargo hold. Nobody loves the smell of *that* in the morning.[3]

So, we've established that elephants, despite their flaws, were highly sought after and seen the incredible lengths taken to get them to the right place at the right time. This leaves the question of how, other than with the driver's hammer and chisel, could you stop the enemy's war elephants? Well, this is where it gets really interesting.

Anti-elephant devices

Elephants, it should now be clear, were formidable combatants, and a wide variety of methods were attempted to counter them, with mixed results.

The direct approach

Remarkably, there were rare instances where a single heroic man could defeat an elephant in hand-to-hand, or rather hand-to-trunk, combat.

At the Battle of Beth Zechariah in 162 BC, the Jewish rebel, Eleazar Maccabeus (fourth son of Matathias and younger brother of Judas Maccabeus, the founder and leading proponent of the Maccabean revolt) thought a particularly well-armoured Seleucid elephant must be carrying King Antiochus V. Determined to strike at the head of the oppressor (or rightful king, depending on your outlook) he charged forward. Hacking left and right he fought his way through the Seleucid formation to the elephant in question and then, in the words of the biblical Book of Maccabees 'he went between the feet of the elephant, and put himself under it: and slew it, and it fell to the ground upon him, and he died there'. [I Maccabees, 6.446]. King Antiochus was not present at the battle, and what the Jewish sources, i.e. the biblical book of Maccabees, do not mention is that the remaining elephants and the rest of the Seleucid army romped on to a clear victory.

During the Battle of Thapsus, which Julius Caesar fought in 46 BC, a veteran of the Fifth Legion single-handedly attacked an elephant while it was busy kneeling on one of his compatriots. When the elephant saw him coming, it grabbed him in its trunk and lifted him high in the air. The Roman faced almost certain death but he was, according to the marvellously understated ancient source 'the kind of man who knew that in a dangerous situation like this determination was required', so he desperately hacked away at the trunk with his sword until he 'caused the beast such pain that it threw him aside and with tremendous noise and flurry rejoined the other elephants'.[4]

These examples aside, armies showed immense ingenuity (sometimes insanity) in devising more devious means of countering elephants.

Faux elephants

Imitation, they say, is the sincerest form of flattery and it is an indication of the impression war elephants made on enemy armies that they soon tried to emulate them. The obvious way to tackle elephants was to get some of your own, fighting fire with fire, but a force of trained elephants is not something you could conjure out of thin air. The next best thing was to convince the enemy you had some when you didn't, or so thought the semi-legendary Queen Semiramis.

Semiramis, as Greek and Roman sources called her, is almost certainly the same person as Sammuramat, Queen of Babylon, the widow of King Shamshi-Adad V who ruled from 810 to 807 BC as regent for her young son, Adad-nirari III (810–783 BC). The Semiramis we know through the Greek writer Diodorus Siculus (who based his account on the earlier Ctesius of Cnidus), was ambitious and ruthless. The king had fallen in love with her after she personally led a commando raid that captured a hitherto-impregnable fortress, and forced her existing husband to commit suicide so he could marry her. The king conveniently died after the birth of their son, leaving her as queen. By another account she was a beautiful courtesan who tricked the king into giving her royal powers for five days. On the first day she threw a big party to gain popularity with the court and generals, then on the second day had the king arrested and imprisoned for life. Either way, Diodorus credits Queen Semiramis with the building of just about everything, including the Hanging Gardens of Babylon. A real feisty 'ball-breaker' as the Americans might say (literally, since she is also credited with being the inventor of eunuchs), she soon tired of building stuff and 'became eager to achieve some great exploit in war'. Noting that India was the largest country in the known world she decided to invade it and set in place a two-year plan to prepare a massive invasion force drawn from all corners of her empire. Her spies told her that the Indian king, Stratobates, had a large force of trained elephants, so Semiramis came up with a cunning plan:

> Observing that she was greatly inferior because of her lack of elephants, Semiramis conceived the plan of making dummies like these animals, in the hope that the Indians would be struck with terror because of their belief that no elephants ever existed at all apart from those found in India. Accordingly, she chose out three hundred thousand black oxen and distributed their meat among her artisans and the men who had been assigned to the task of making the figures, but the hides she sewed together and stuffed with straw, and thus made dummies, copying in every detail the natural appearance of these animals. Each dummy had with it a man to take care of it and a camel and, when it was moved by the latter, to those who saw it from a distance it looked like an actual animal.
>
> [Diodorus, *Bibliotheke*, II.16.8]

The likeliest explanation is that these were not solid dummies, but coverings of leather, padded out with straw in the appropriate places, that the camels actually wore as a disguise. Great secrecy surrounded their construction and further care was then taken to have her own cavalry immunized 'by bringing their horses up to these camels, [and so] accustomed them not to fear the savage nature of the beasts'.

Happy with her preparations, and laughing off Stratobates' threats to crucify her if she attacked, Semiramis led her assembled army out from Balkh in Afghanistan and began the invasion. Her army crossed a pontoon bridge over the Indus River, 'the dummy elephants leading the way in order that the king's spies might report to the king the multitude of these animals in her army'. Remarkably the ruse worked, and Stratobates was dumbfounded as to where his enemy had got these elephants from and, fearing his key advantage was neutralized, retreated. Soon, however, some

14

deserters from Semiramis' army spilled the beans and the Indians with their real elephants turned to give battle.

Even with the camel out of the bag, so to speak, the fake elephants still almost secured a victory for Semiramis. Stratobates, now full of renewed confidence, sent his cavalry and chariot forces into attack while he was still coming up with the elephants and infantry. Semiramis had deployed the dummy elephants spread out at intervals in front of her main line as a screen. Now, although the Indian horses were familiar with elephants and so made their approach run undaunted, these elephants did not look quite right up close and stank of camel, which the horses were not used to, and caused them to screech to a halt, some throwing their riders while others bolted back through the infantry coming up behind. Amidst this confusion Semiramis led an attack with her elite troops that completed the rout of the remaining Indian cavalry and chariots. So far so good for the disguised camels, but the game was up as soon as Stratobates, 'fighting from the most powerful of the beasts', led his real elephants in to the attack. The imposters were no match for the real thing and were quickly destroyed along with the rest of the army 'some being trampled beneath their feet, others ripped up by their tusks, and a number tossed into the air by their trunks'.

The survivors fled back across the pontoon bridge, which fortunately broke just after a wounded Semiramis had got across. Sometime after, the warrior queen mysteriously disappeared, following a plot by her son and a disgruntled eunuch.

Semiramis' disguised camels, which had worked better than one might expect, were not the last case of fake elephants. Visitors to the Royal Palace at Uidapur in India can see a display dedicated to Maharana Pratap and his horse Chatak. The display includes a life-sized model of Chatak, complete with the fake elephant trunk he apparently wore in Pratap's fateful last battle at Haldighati in 1576. Pratap was resisting the expansionist Mughal ruler Akbar, whose army included numerous sword-wielding elephants. Chatak's disguise was meant to confuse the elephants who might mistake him for a baby elephant, allowing him to get close to them unmolested. It worked in so far as Pratap was able to get close enough to attack the Mughal commander, Man Singh. Chatak apparently reared up in front of Singh's personal elephant and smashed his hooves on its trunk, while Pratap thrust with his lance at Singh. Unfortunately, the blow missed its mark, though it did kill the mahout. The elephant, or another nearby, then swung with the sword held in its trunk and seriously wounded brave Chatak. Pratap too was soon wounded, but Chatak managed to bear him away to safety before dying.

Dummy elephants were used by King Perseus of Macedon when he rebelled against his Roman overlords in 171 BC. Knowing the Roman army coming against him contained some elephants (those we met earlier, sliding downhill on their rumps) and mindful of the damage that such animals had caused to his father's army at the Battle of Cynoscephelae (197 BC), he was determined to come up with an effective counter. He sought to protect his own cavalry from the terror that elephants often induced in such troops, which was in part at least due to the horses' distaste for the pachyderms' smell. According to Dio:

> Also, in order to make sure that the beasts should not prove a source of terror to the horses, he constructed images of elephants and smeared them with some kind of ointment to give them a dreadful odour. They were terrible both to see and to hear, since they were skilfully arranged to emit a roar resembling thunder; and he would repeatedly lead the horses up to these figures until they gained courage.
>
> [Dio, *Roman History*, XX]

These dummy elephants were only used as a training method, not intended to actually fool the enemy like Semiramis' disguised camels. Actually quite a sensible precaution, they should help to prevent fear in his own cavalry, but would not in themselves harm the enemy. For this he relied on another scheme.

Perseus' living anti-tank minefield

One of the ways in which the analogy of elephants and modern tanks holds up well is that they shared a common weakness in their means of locomotion. Just as the weakpoint of a tank was its tracks, so the elephant's was in his feet. Although a 'pachyderm', i.e. literally thick-skinned, and therefore possessed of a degree of natural armour all over its body, the elephant has surprisingly delicate soles to its feet. Mind you, your feet would probably be pretty tender if you weighed four tons.

This chink in the elephant's armour was identified pretty early on and various simple but effective measures were employed by armies expecting to face the beasts in battle. At the Siege of Megalopolis in 318 BC, the defenders had triumphed by burying spiked beams inside the breach in the wall through which they expected Polyperchon's elephants to storm. At the Battle of Gaza in 312 BC, the army of Ptolemy I deployed 'the men who were to handle the spiked devices made of iron and connected by chains that they had prepared' opposite the massed elephants of Demetrius Poliorcetes' right wing. In both cases many elephants were injured when their mahouts tried to drive them across the booby-trapped area. At Megalopolis they turned back in pain and confusion and crashed through their own army with the usual devastating results, while at Gaza, unsure whether to advance or retreat, they milled around while their mahouts were picked off with arrows and javelins and the beasts themselves were then captured. At Asculum in 279 BC the Roman countermeasures included caltrops, iron devices shaped like the jacks used in the traditional children's game so that however they were thrown down at least one spike was always pointing up. These measures were effectively the first anti-tank minefields, but like later minefields they required some preparation and basically relied on the enemy elephants attacking in the right place. Once spiked chains or heavy timber frames were deployed, or caltrops scattered, they could not easily be taken up again in the heat of battle and redeployed elsewhere. What Perseus needed was something spiky, yet mobile.

The answer he came up with was a specially-equipped corps of *elephantomachoi* (elephant fighters). Their special equipment? Spiky armour and helmets so that any elephant treading on them would hopefully hurt their delicate tootsies. One can only imagine how this concept was sold to the troops involved. 'So, my Lord, I love the new armour, but could you just tell me again what the spikes are for?'

When Perseus finally met the Romans and their elephants (those that had skidded down the mountainsides on their rumps) in open battle near Pydna in 168 BC, this special corps failed. They made such a slight impression that Livy's account of the battle merely records 'on this occasion the "anti-elephant corps" was a mere name without any practical utility'. [Livy, XLIV.41]

Anti-elephant wagons

After suffering a traumatic defeat at the hands (and trunks) of Pyrrhus of Epirus in 280 BC, in which his war elephants played a significant part, the Romans put some thought into their game plan for the rematch the following year at Asculum. According to Dionysius of Halicarnassus, this is what they came up with:

> Outside the line they stationed the light-armed troops and the waggons, three hundred in number, which they had got ready for the battle against the elephants. These wagons had upright beams on which were mounted movable traverse poles that could be swung round as quick as thought in any direction one might wish, and on the ends of the poles there were either tridents or sword-like spikes or scythes all of iron; or again they had cranes that hurled down heavy grappling-irons. Many of the poles had attached to them and projecting in front of the wagons fire-bearing grapnels wrapped in tow that had been liberally daubed with pitch, which men standing on the wagons were to set afire as soon as they came near the elephants and then rain blows with them upon the trunks and faces of the beasts. Furthermore, standing on the wagons, which were four-wheeled, were many also of the light-armed troops – bowmen, hurlers of stones and slingers who threw iron caltrops; and on the ground beside the wagons there were still more men
> [Dionysius of Halicarnassus, *Roman Antiquities*, XX.1]

In the ensuing battle these wagons, it seems, did okay at first. When Pyrrhus committed his elephants at a point of crisis, the wagons were successfully moved to meet them and at first succeeded in blocking their advance. However, the elephants' drivers had them stand off while the crews in their howdahs pelted the wagons with javelins and arrows and Pyrrhus' light infantry (detachments of which usually accompanied each elephant) simply hamstrung the oxen pulling the wagons and thus immobilized them. The elephants then resumed their attack on the main Roman line, which, as noted earlier, ran away as if from a tidal wave. Pyrrhus had won but, although no more than one or two of his elephants were killed, his other losses were so heavy that he is supposed to have said 'one more victory like that over the Romans will destroy us completely', thus giving us the phrase 'Pyrrhic victory'.

Hogs of war
Polyaenus' book of stratagems contains this gem, relating to the attack by Antigonus of Macedon on Megara in central Greece in 266 BC.

> At the siege of Megara, Antigonus brought his elephants into the attack; but the Megarians daubed some swine with pitch, set fire to it, and let them loose among the elephants. The pigs grunted and shrieked under the torture of the fire, and sprang forwards as hard as they could among the elephants, who broke their ranks in confusion and fright, and ran off in different directions. From this time onwards, Antigonus ordered the Indians, when they trained up their elephants, to bring up swine among them; so that the elephants might thus become accustomed to the sight of them, and to their noise.
>
> [Polyaenus, *Stratagems*, IV.6.3]

I need add nothing.

Tamerlane's bullring
When Timur i-lenk, better known as Timur the Lame or Tamerlane, invaded Indian in 1398, his Turkish troops were very apprehensive about meeting the enemy's numerous war elephants. To reassure them he fortified his camp with an outer ring of sharp stakes and an inner ring formed of live buffaloes (these accompanied armies both as draught animals and as meat on the hoof) tied head to tail. To the horns of each were tied bundles of dried brambles. The plan was that in the event of an attack by enemy elephants, the brambles would be lit and the flames and agonized bellows of the cattle would terrify the elephants.[5]

Smoking camels can damage your health

A similar trick, also attributed to Tamerlane was to tie bundles of straw to the saddles of camels. When enemy elephants approached, the straw would be lit and the terrified, smoking camels would be driven towards the elephants in the hope of causing them to panic and stampede among their own troops.

A well-balanced force

Some Indian armies of the Mughal period apparently contained swordsmen trained to walk on stilts, giving them the height to reach and attack the mahouts of enemy elephants. Britons, the famous maker of traditional toy soldiers, even made a model of such a warrior. The stilts, obviously, were strapped to the warriors legs, leaving his hands free to wield his weapons. It is easy to imagine one of these plucky chaps being swatted by an elephant and taking down a row of his comrades like dominoes.[6]

Chinese lions used to scare elephants

At the siege of Qusu in China in AD 446, the attackers made bamboo lions which apparently panicked the elephants within the town into running amok among the defenders.[7]

Shaggy elephant story

Before I leave the subject of elephants, I must just mention the case of Gujar Khan, who fought the Mughals in sixteenth-century India. Knowing Mughal cavalry horses were well accustomed to elephants, he disguised his elephants as giant yaks, using coverings made of their shaggy coats stitched together. The horses of the enemy were terrified by this new creature and fled.[8]

Chapter 2

Ignominious Deaths

Throughout military history, professional warriors have dreamed that, if they cannot survive, they might at least be granted a heroic death in battle, worthy of song and remembrance. Military literature is liberally sprinkled with eloquent statements of intent to meet death in manly fashion. A Spartan once said that for a man neither life nor death should be ends in themselves, but to accomplish both nobly was a worthy aim. The Gurkhas pledged themselves to death before dishonour. Some warriors, however, are cruelly (but often amusingly with hindsight) denied such glory.

Cambyses, Persian slipper

Cambyses, the Great King of Persia, was on his way home after conquering Egypt and making a nuisance of himself there for several years (just little things like killing the Apis bull which the Egyptians revered as a living god, that sort of thing). He was passing through Syria when he learnt that a coup had undermined his power back home. Being a man of action and intending to set off without delay to challenge the usurper, Cambyses immediately went to vault onto his horse. Unfortunately he made a bit of a mess of it and got entangled with his sword. The chape of his sword's sheath (the cap that closes the end) chose this moment to fall off and the point of the blade pierced Cambyses' thigh. He died some twenty days later from the effects of gangrene, a ghastly death he thoroughly deserved since he was a nasty little chap. He left no heirs since he had murdered most of his relatives, including his brother and one of the two sisters he had incestuously married, who was pregnant with his heir at the time.

The death of Uesugi Kenshin – short and to the point

No culture had a greater sense of the idea of a fitting death than the samurai of feudal Japan. One samurai encapsulated the way of the warrior, *bushido*, when he wrote:

> As long as it is my duty towards my lord, I would like to die in battle in front of his eyes. If I die in my home, it will be a death without significance.   [Okuba Tadataka, 1622]

Such was the culture into which Uesugi Kenshin was born in Echigo province in 1530 though his given name was Nagao Kagetora. After his father died in battle he was sent at the age of seven to a buddhist monastery. He left it aged fourteen and began leading missions against his family's enemies. He earnt such a military reputation that within a few years he was elevated above his older brother as head of his family. When he was still just twenty-one, the leader of the Uesugi clan (the Nagao family's overlords), adopted him as his heir and made him Lord of Echigo province. He thus became Uesugi Kagetora and later, when he took religious vows and the Buddhist personal name Kenshin, he was Uesugi Kenshin, the name by which he is usually known to history.

Kenshin was a samurai's samurai. His swords, the most famous of which is preserved with great reverence in Japan, had no hand-guard, so that nobody might accuse him of being afraid of injury. His courage in battle is exemplified by his conduct at the Fourth Battle of Kawanakajima (18 October 1561). There were five battles of Kawanakajima, all of them fought between Kenshin and his arch-enemy, Takeda Shingen, ruler of the province of Kai. On this occasion, Kenshin personally charged on horseback into Shingen's curtained command enclosure in an effort to settle the matter man-to-man (incidentally his horse was wearing cloth slippers to muffle the sound of its approach). Shingen, another Buddhist monk, defended himself with an iron war fan (yes, that is a fan that doubled as a weapon of last resort) until Kenshin's horse bolted and carried him back to his own lines.

Having proved himself a paragon of warrior virtue by such exploits, Kenshin would have hoped and expected to die sword in hand, facing a worthy enemy. Sadly, as it turned out, he never got to look his nemesis in the eye. Not only was his killer a midget, reputedly less than 3 feet tall, but he struck Kenshin from a wholly unexpected direction. On 12 April 1578, Ukifune Jinnai was one of a group of ninja that infiltrated Kenshin's headquarters, killing most of his guards (themselves ninja) with poisonous darts fired from blowguns. While Jinnai's accomplices were hunted down and killed by the heroic efforts of the one surviving guard, the half-pint assassin hid himself in the cesspit below Kenshin's personal latrine. His blowpipe probably came in handy as a snorkel as he settled in for the night. This may have been the plan all along, the rest a mere diversion. Either that or he just got lucky (sic!). In either case, when Kenshin came next morning to empty his bowels, Jinnai filled them again with an upward thrust of his spear. Kenshin died of his wounds four days later.

In case you are wondering, the ninja was probably sent by the ruthless and ambitious Oda Nobunaga. It was certainly not down to Kenshin's old rival, Takeda Shingen, as he had already been killed by a drunken sniper at the siege of Noda in 1573 while peering over the battlements to better appreciate some pretty flute music emanating from the enemy camp.

The grand ~~entrance~~ exit of Gautier d'Autreche

The knights of Western Europe lived by a very similar set of ideals to the Japanese samurai. Their biggest preoccupation was in demonstrating their skill at arms and gaining a reputation as a brave and honourable warrior. In particular, although a knight might fight on foot when tactics demanded it, it was at mounted combat that excellence was most sought. In every major European language apart from English, the word for a knight actually means 'horseman' (French *chevalier*, Spanish *caballero*, German *Ritter* etc.) and the oft-misunderstood code of 'chivalry' really just means acting in the manner befitting an aristocratic horseman. This warrior ethic did tend to exist in tension with the parallel demands that a knight also be a good Christian. For many, the Crusades offered the ideal solution to this dilemma, since a knight could, by chopping up the heathen 'Saracens', simultaneously demonstrate his martial prowess and do the Lord's work, showing what a nice, pure Christian he was. The chance to grab some land and loot didn't discourage the Crusading spirit either.

One such paragon of Christian chivalry was Gautier d'Autreche, lord of Castillon in central France. He joined the Seventh Crusade under King Louis IX (St Louis as he was to become – killing Saracens being no bar to sainthood). Louis' expedition was aimed at Egypt and his forces made an opposed landing at Damietta in the Nile delta. They fought their way ashore but were pretty soon bogged down and virtually besieged in their encampment by surrounding Saracen forces. Louis gave orders for his knights to stay in their pavilions, remain patient and not do anything rash until a proper response could be devised. (Actually Louis spent a lot of his time in his tent anyway as he, like many of his unfortunate army, was beset with dysentery so bad that 'it became necessary to cut away the lower part of his drawers'.) Gautier, however, decided that honour and pride demanded otherwise.

Determined to make a name for himself, he had his war horse brought into his pavilion and decked out in its trappings bearing his family coat of arms. He had his squires help him into his full armour, his surcoat similarly declaring his identity for all to see, then mounted his horse. When all was ready he had the flaps to his pavilion thrown back and his assembled servants, to ensure everyone was watching, gave a rousing cheer. So far, so good for bold, brave Sir Gautier as he rode out resplendent under the eyes of his peers, put spur to horse and set off on his single-handed dash towards the Saracen lines.

Unfortunately, before he reached the enemy lines he lost control of his horse and fell off. According to Jean of Joinville, whose eyewitness account in his *Life of St Louis* is the key source for this Crusade, this 'was because the Saracens, for the most part, were mounted on mares, and the stallion was consequently attracted to their side'. Gautier's randy steed 'leapt over his body and went careering forward, still covered with its master's arms, right into the midst of our enemies'. To add injury to insult, 'four Turks came rushing towards my lord Gautier as he lay on the ground, and aimed great blows with their maces at his body as they went by'.

The constable of France and some men-at-arms came to the rescue and managed to carry poor Gautier back to the relative safety of the camp, but his troubles were not yet over. He was now at the mercy of the notoriously inept Western medicine of this period (better for him if he had been taken prisoner by the Turks). Joinville recounts:

> Several of the army surgeons and physicians went to see him, and because he did not seem to them to be in danger of dying, they bled him in both arms.

Joinville himself visited his stricken comrade in his tent later that day but found him dead. He does not record whether Gautier died from his initial injuries, the inept efforts of the quacks or sheer embarrassment.

So Gautier did not reach Jerusalem, but at least he got closer than some others who 'took the cross'. Joinville records how one unfortunate missed the boat to military glory during the army's earlier beach assault at Damietta. Knights were crossing from their ships to shallower-draught galleys which would then be run aground on the beach to deliver them ashore. One fellow stepped over the side, only to find the galley had already pulled away. Encased in full armour he plunged straight to the bottom. Not that funny in its own right, maybe, but I simply had to include it as the knight had the delightful name of Plonquet. We might also spare a thought for a group of warriors who followed Richard I (the Lionheart) on the Third Crusade. Their quest for spiritual salvation, fighting and loot got no further than Cyprus, where they were crushed beneath a toppling pile of grain stockpiled to feed the army – proving that wholemeal is not always good for your health.

Bitten to death by a dead foe – the bizarre end of Sigurd the Mighty

If Uesugi Kenshin's death was squalid and Gautier d'Autreche's farcical, Sigurd Eysteinsson's was simply bizarre. Sigurd, also known as Sigurd the Mighty, was of good Viking stock and was Earl of Orkney from 875–892 or thereabouts, with lands also in Caithness on the Scottish mainland. Here his borders were the source of friction with his Pictish neighbour, Máel Brigte, or Máel the Bucktoothed, who held lands in Moray to the south.

To settle their long-running dispute once and for all, Sigurd challenged Máel to a formal massed duel, both agreeing to meet at the appointed place (probably near Dornoch) with forty men each. Ritualized, judicial combat in various forms was common in many Northern European societies. The general idea seems to have been that the fight placed the dispute under the eyes of the gods (or God once those societies were Christianized), who would not let the wrong side prevail. Sigurd clearly didn't feel too sure of divine sympathy for his cause as he decided on a little insurance policy in the form of an extra forty men. To his credit, Máel did not flee when he discovered this treachery, instead resolving to go down fighting (or perhaps hoping to kill Sigurd in any case). Unsurprisingly, he and his men were swiftly overwhelmed. The triumphant Sigurd cut off Máel's head and hung it from his saddle to take it home as a trophy and proof of his victory.

Sigurd seemed to have got the verdict he wanted but the true justice was about to be done. As he rode, he accidentally kicked his leg against the buck teeth of Máel's severed head, breaking the skin. The wound became infected and he died some time after, probably from tetanus or septicaemia, either one of which would have been a nasty way to go.

'Hi Homey, I'm a Hun'

Attila, who became sole leader of the Huns in the 430s after (probably) murdering his brother Bleda, is one of the most infamous warlords of the ancient period. For two decades, the 'scourge of God' and his army of Huns and assorted other barbarians bullied the Romans into paying them annual tribute to leave them alone, but invaded anyway. His last great invasion of the Western Empire in 451 briefly extended his empire from its powerbase on the Hungarian plain, to within a day's ride of the Atlantic Ocean. His death in 453 came, however, not from wounds suffered in one of his many battles, but in his marital bed on his wedding night. Having drunk excessive amounts of alcohol he choked on his own blood, traditionally explained as a nose bleed, but possibly from rupture of oesophageal varices, essentially a condition like haemorrhoids but at the lower end of the throat. This is apparently the top cause of death for chronic alcoholics.

The sad death of Charles Wooden VC

Charles Wooden earned immortality when he won the Victoria Cross for his actions in the famous charge of the Light Brigade at the Battle of Balaklava in 1854. Having had his horse shot from under him in the early stages of the charge and trudged back to the relative safety of the British lines, Sergeant Major Wooden ventured back into 'the valley of death' to help Surgeon James Mouat rescue the wounded Captain William Morris. Never mind that he had to wait four years to get his VC, and then only got it because he complained that Mouat had got one and he hadn't, Wooden was a hero and had the medal to prove it. By then he had also served through the Indian Mutiny and did not return to England until posted to Dover in 1871, settling into garrison life with his wife and children.

There was, however, to be no peaceful end for this hero. In late April 1875 Lieutenant Wooden, as he now was, began complaining of severe headaches but carried on with his duties. On 25 April the regimental medical officer was summoned to Wooden's quarters where his batman (a soldier who acts as personal valet to an officer, not a caped crime-fighter) informed the doctor that the lieutenant was bleeding profusely from the nose and mouth and complaining that he had a tooth that needed extracting. Entering the room, the doctor found that Lieutenant Wooden had clearly been drinking heavily and had severe damage to the roof of his mouth. Two spent cartridges were lying on the floor and Mrs Wooden admitted to having removed a pistol before the doctor arrived. Lieutenant Wooden died some twelve hours later, the subsequent inquest recording a verdict of 'temporary insanity'.[9]

You Canute be serious! The inglorious end of Edmund Ironsides

Sources record two traditions regarding the death of Edmund 'Ironsides'. Neither was quite the end hoped for by this warrior king of Wessex who thrice defeated the Danish Canute only to be defeated through treachery in a fourth battle at Ashingdon in AD 1016. Defeat at that battle forced Edmund to agree to a partition of England in which he retained Wessex but Canute (he who famously tried to command the tide to turn back) got the rest. A short while later, Edmund was assassinated, either hacked to death as he sat on a latrine or killed by a booby-trapped statue sent to him as a gift, which released a small, spring-loaded and poisoned sword. Either way, agents of King Canute are suspected and the devious Dane soon became king of all England.[10]

Trophy emperor

For the Roman Emperor Valentinian, it was not so much the actual moment of death that was inglorious as his circumstances immediately before and after it. It was shameful enough for a Roman emperor to be taken alive by the enemy, as Valentinian was by the Persian King Shapur I in 260, but to then be forced to serve as his mounting block must have been unimaginably hard to bear. Thereafter, whenever Shapur wanted to mount his horse, he would first step on the neck of the crouching Valentinian. Even death, when it finally came two long years later, was not the end of the shame since Shapur had his flayed skin stuffed with straw and displayed in a temple as a trophy. Apparently it was brought out and gloatingly shown to visiting Roman diplomats for centuries after.

Dive, dive ... oh, no wait a minute!

U-boat skipper, Kapitänleutnant Rolf Mützelburg was one of the star commanders of Germany's 1st U-boat Flotilla. A very experienced submariner by September 1942, he had survived seven patrols in which his boat, U-203 had sunk nineteen ships and damaged three others, for which feats he had been awarded the Knight's Cross and Oak Leaves. On 11 September 1942, while his U-203 was surfaced, he decided to take the opportunity to get some exercise by going for a swim. Diving from the conning tower he managed to miss all of the surrounding Atlantic ocean and instead hit the deck of the U-boat head-first and was killed.[11]

Chapter 3

What's in a Name?

Strangest names for weapons

Cat-scrapper (or *Katzbalger* in German): the sword carried as a side-arm by *landscknechts* (German mercenary infantry) in the fifteenth and sixteenth centuries.

Iklwa: the Zulu short stabbing spear, apparently named for the squelching, sucking sound it made as it was pulled out from an enemy's belly.

Bohemian ear spoon (or *Böhmischer Ohrlöffel* in German): a type of late-medieval spear with an additional point projecting laterally on either side of the main spear head.

Puckle gun: Invented in 1718, this was actually an idea ahead of its time. It was a tripod-mounted, repeating flintlock musket or small cannon (with a 37mm bore) which could fire nine rounds a minute (compared to the two or three rounds per minute a trained infantry-man could fire from his musket). It came in two versions, one firing round bullets and the other square-section bullets. According to the patent, the latter was intended for use against Muslims since the blunt projectiles would do more damage and convince them 'of the benefits of Christian civilization'.

HMS *Pickle*: a schooner, was the second smallest ship in Nelson's fleet at Trafalgar.

Godendag: A heavy cudgel with large iron spikes favoured by the rebellious Flemish peasantry in the Middle Ages. Its finest hour was the defeat of the French noble cavalry at the Battle of Courtrai in 1302. A serious weapon, it becomes funny when you realize the name means 'Good day' which is apparently what the revolting peasants would say as they used it to bash the brains out of their betters.

Bollock knife: A medieval knife with a bulbous lobe either side of the blade.

Bastard sword: A large medieval sword that could be used either one or two handed.

Arse girdle: Not actually a weapon but the low-slung sword belt worn by medieval knights. This is the contemporary term, but prudish later historians invented the more delicate term 'belt of plates' for it.

Hitler's mechanical menagerie

For all their detestable qualities, it has to be admitted that the Nazis did know how to choose suitably ferocious sounding names for their military kit. Many of their tanks and other armoured fighting vehicles were named after feline predators or other tough and dangerous beasts. For example:

Leopard (VK1602 reconnaissance tank; scrapped at prototype stage, the name was too good to waste and was recycled for post-war West Germany's main battle tank)
Puma
Lynx
Panther
Tiger (the most famous of all)
Bison
Brummbär (Grizzly Bear – the Sturmpanzer IV)
Nashorn (Rhinoceros)
Elefant (work it out)

Okay, so it went a bit soft with the Hummel (Bumble Bee). Apart from sounding comical, the name of a creature that can only sting once and then must die can hardly have inspired confidence in the crew.

Surprisingly, where the Germans showed a sense of ironic humour in their tank names was when the Reich was already crumbling around their ears. The Maus (Mouse) was a 188-tonne monster of which only two prototypes were made before the war's end (but we'll hear more of Maus later).

30

British and Commonwealth forces occasionally looked to the animal kingdom for inspiration too, but never really got the hang of making them sound impressive:

Crab
Locust
Kangaroo
Dingo
Ram
Tortoise (which never got past prototype stage)
Firefly

Only the variant of the Churchill tank known as the Crocodile sounded vaguely scary but this was still an odd choice for a vehicle that was not remotely aquatic. It was actually the flame-throwing variant, so Dragon would have been a more obvious choice. Perhaps this image problem was only to be expected from a nation whose early tank doctrine included a defensive tactic in which concealed tanks were to emerge from their hiding places 'like savage rabbits'.

The unofficial nicknames awarded to tanks by their crews are often more revealing. The M4 Sherman was a war-winner for the Allies, largely through the virtue of being easy to build in huge numbers, but its petrol engine had a terrible habit of bursting into flames easily when hit, often incinerating its crew. This earned it the unofficial nickname of the 'Ronson', after the famous cigarette lighters whose marketing tag line was 'lights first time, every time'. Another American tank, the M3 Medium Tank did not overly impress the Russian tank crews to whom they were sent in large numbers under the 'lend-lease' scheme. They rather ungratefully labelled it the 'coffin for six brothers'. By contrast, when the home-grown SU-152 entered service in late 1943, the Russians were so pleased with its effectiveness against the Germans' feared Panthers and Tigers that they swiftly dubbed it *Zveroboy* (Beasthunter).

Chapter 4

A Misplaced Sense of Honour

Hey! It's my turn

The ancient Chinese chronicle known as the *Tso Chuan* relates an event that occurred in 520 BC during a battle between Hua and Tsin, two of the many states of pre-unification China. One feature of warfare at the time was aristocrats galloping around in chariots taking pot shots at each other with bows. P'ao of Hua managed to get close enough for a shot at the Tsin general, Shing, but missed. Quickly reloading, P'ao was about to shoot again when his target protested that it would be unchivalrous to shoot twice before he had himself taken a shot in reply. Not wanting to be thought rude, P'ao lowered his bow and allowed Shing to take his first shot unhurried. P'ao was killed instantly.[12]

A promise is a promise

During the First Punic War, the Roman consul, Marcus Atilius Regulus, was sent with an army to fight the Carthaginians on their North African doorstep. His army was crushed in battle (many of them quite literally by a massed elephant charge) and he was himself taken prisoner. Thinking they had taught the Romans a lesson and wanting to negotiate from a position of strength, the Carthaginians offered Regulus the chance to return to Rome to deliver their conditions for peace to the Roman Senate. Regulus had to swear an oath to speak in favour of accepting peace on the Carthaginian terms and to return to Carthage if the Senate refused.

Regulus returned to Rome in 250 BC and delivered the Carthaginian demands to the Senate. True to his word, he first spoke in favour of accepting the humiliating terms (any peace that they

32

didn't dictate over the smoking ruins of the enemy's homes was humiliating to the Romans) and the demoralized Senate, so the story goes, was on the verge of accepting them. Regulus then delivered a fiery speech against making peace with the Carthaginians and the Senate voted to continue the war. Ignoring the pleas of his friends to remain in Rome, Regulus then returned to Carthage as promised and was tortured to death.[13]

Premature decapitation

At the Fourth Battle of Kawanakajima in 1567, one-legged samurai general Yamamoto Kansuke was on the command staff of Takeda Shingen's army, which faced that of Uesugi Kenshin (of midget ninja fame). Hopping mad that the battle seemed to be going badly, Kansuke decided to commit *hara kiri* (ritual suicide) rather than face the shame of defeat and having let his master down. The ritual of *seppuku* (self disembowelment with his sword, followed by an attendant lopping off his head) was duly carried out. Unfortunately, he had been too pessimistic as his side went on to win the battle.[14]

The one that got away

Captain Patrick Ferguson, a regular officer in the army of George III, may be considered a doyen of the art of military sniping. After all, he contributed greatly by inventing the Ferguson Rifle which was lighter, more accurate and more rapid to fire than the standard smoothbore Brown Bess musket of the day. Having demonstrated the weapon's excellent qualities, Ferguson was sent off to North America (where the American rebellion against their rightful king was hotting up) with a royal commission to lead a unit of sharp-shooters that was to be specially formed to use his rifle.

The unit was soon giving good service but an incident on 3 September 1777 suggests that Ferguson, while a thoroughly decent chap, lacked the ruthlessness now considered essential in a sniper. Ferguson and three of his sharpshooters were reconnoitring along the Brandywine Creek when they heard horses approaching and took up ambush positions with rifles levelled. Two riders appeared, one in the uniform of a senior officer of the Continental Army (i.e. American rebel army). According to Ferguson's own letters, he initially ordered his men to 'steal near to them and fire at them' but then decided it was dashed unsporting to shoot a chap who didn't even know he was there and countermanded the order. Stepping out from cover, he invited the horsemen to dismount and be taken prisoner but, rather rudely, they turned and rode off. Even then a word from Ferguson would have seen the riders cut down in an instant but he felt 'it was not pleasant to fire at the back of an unoffending individual who was acquitting himself coolly of his duty, and so I let him alone'.[15]

Four days later Ferguson was wounded at the Battle of Brandy-wine Creek (a British victory) and it was while recovering in hospital that he learned that the senior officer he had encountered was none other than George Washington, commander-in-chief of the Continental Army. The other rider, in case you are curious, was just one of those many officers sent by the interfering French as part of the intervention that tipped the balance and enabled the rebels to win (though they were not yet officially at war with England). Even with hindsight Ferguson wrote in January 1778: 'I am not sorry that I did not know all the time who it was'. Washington, of course went on to win the war and secure US independence. By contrast, Ferguson, by then a Major, was killed in action at the Battle of King's Mountain where, according to some reports, his gallant enemies stripped his corpse and urinated on it. God bless America!

No, I insist, after *you*

At the Battle of Fontenoy in 1745, the so-called Pragmatic Army (an alliance of British, Dutch, Austrians and others) faced a presumably-doctrinaire French army near the River Scheldt. At the height of the battle, the First Foot Guards led a column of British infantry uphill against the enemy position, bayonets fixed, muskets primed and ready to fire, meticulously closing the gaps torn in their nice neat ranks by enemy cannon balls. Reaching the top of the slope they found themselves face to face with the Gardes Françaises, a regiment they had helped put to flight at the Battle of Dettingen two years previously. Both sides halted. Captain Lord Charles Hay politely doffed his cap and the French commander reciprocated. As the rank and file no doubt eyed each other somewhat nervously,

Hay took out his hip flask and raised a toast to the French, his men responding with three cheers. He informed his enemy counterpart that his men intended to make the French guards flee and swim the Scheldt as they had made them swim the Main at Dettingen, then said something along the lines of 'Sir, be good enough to fire first'.

The Frenchman politely declined: 'Gentlemen, we never fire first, fire yourselves'. The British still held their fire, while the Third Foot Guards, next in the column, moved up on their flanks to extend the firing line and small cannon ('battalion guns') were readied. French nerve broke first, sending a volley crashing into the red-coated British ranks. While the French were furiously reloading (a very slow process with smoothbore muskets), the surviving guards reordered their ranks, fired a disciplined volley with muskets and battalion guns together and steamed in with the bayonet, sending the Gardes Françaises fleeing to the rear.

Chapter 5

Suicide Mission

With a little help from my friends

Mithridates VI (the Great) of Pontus, was an implacable enemy of the Romans, whom he fought in several wars in the early first century BC. He could even claim to have won one of these wars, a rare achievement. He carved a fair-sized empire for himself around the Black Sea, which inevitably involved the usual (for a megalomaniac monarch) mix of murder (including his own mother and brother), execution, conquest and general ruthlessness, so he was not without a few enemies and his court was a hotbed of conspiracy. Mithridates wasn't averse to the occasional poisoning, but was also justifiably paranoid about assassination attempts on himself. As a precaution he regularly drank special concoctions, including small doses of actual poisons, designed to make himself immune to their effects. Smart plan.

By 63 BC, however, it had all gone pear shaped. Having had several armies defeated and his empire dismantled by the Romans, he found himself trapped in his palace with a rebellious army led by his own son banging on the door. He decided to kill himself rather than be the main attraction in a Roman triumphal parade but had something of a senior moment (he was almost seventy) and chose to use poison. Two daughters, remaining loyal, insisted on taking the deadly potion with him and duly died in front of his eyes, but Mithridates remained unaffected. In the end he had to beg his Celtic bodyguard to polish him off with his sword.

The first cut is the deepest

The samurai Nitta Yoshisada, in a battle against the troublesome monks of Fukishima in 1338, avoided falling into the hands of his enemies by decapitating himself with a single blow. This spectacular feat was rendered all the more impressive by the fact that Yoshisada was not only pinned beneath his wounded horse at the time, but already had an enemy arrow lodged in his forehead.[16]

Yueh time has come

Before unification, China was a mosaic of smaller states with funny names that were more or less constantly at war with each other. All manner of dirty tricks were tried to get the upper hand, but one stands out as simply despicable, The army of Wu was drawn up opposite their Yueh enemies, ready for battle. As the Wu watched, three ranks of men marched forward into the space between the two battle lines and halted. They then drew their swords and one by one began to cut their own throats. Bemused and captivated by this grim and unexpected spectacle, they did not notice other Yueh troops marching round their flank until it was too late and they were easily overrun and defeated. What the Wu hadn't known is that the suicidal troops were actually convicted criminals who were given swords and told to commit suicide as ordered if they wanted their families to be spared death or worse.[17]

Mark 1 minesweeper

In the absence of more sophisticated mine-clearing equipment, the Soviets in the Second World War often ordered penal battalions, that is soldiers convicted of some offence, to charge across suspected or known minefields to clear a path for the troops behind. NKVD military police acted as 'blocking troops' behind to machine-gun any of their own troops who hesitated. To end up in a penal battalion, it was only necessary to be accused of 'defeatist or unpatriotic' behaviour such as trying to withdraw to avoid encirclement or suggesting that communist egalitarianism might have stretched to providing a rifle for every soldier. Communist commanders' rational explanation for such tactics does actually make a crude if callous kind of sense. The minefield was still an enemy position and they probably suffered no more casualties crossing it this way than in a frontal assault on a position the Germans had decided to defend heavily with actual troops. Moreover, it robbed German minefields of their chief tactical function, which was to channel the movements of the enemy into heavily-defended killing zones. Well, that's alright then.

Close call for God's official historian

During the first century AD the Romans were discovering the hard way that Palestine was a hotbed of religious extremism and violence (this was way back in the day, when things were different of course). In AD 69, the Jews were openly revolting against Roman rule and the Romans had sent an army to punish them. At Jotapata, the Romans, who by this period were pretty used to easy victories, had a much tougher fight to get into the city than they expected, thanks to the Jews' fanatical resistance under the inspirational leadership of Josephus. After forty-seven days of artillery bombardment, bloody assaults and various other techniques had failed, the Romans finally got to the last trick in the book and climbed over the walls when all the defenders were asleep and captured the town. By this time the Roman commander, none other than the future Emperor Vespasian, was so full of respect for Josephus' obvious genius and courage (we know this because Josephus' own account tells us so) that he gave his men orders to take Josephus alive. Everyone else was to be killed and the city razed.

The Romans (those great exemplars of European civilization), spent two days scouring the city, killing or enslaving (but generally killing) any men, women and children they could find. Many Jews, intent on a final act of defiance, committed suicide to deprive the Romans of the pleasure. Eventually, thanks to a tip-off from a woman (probably extracted under torture) they found Josephus barricaded in an underground bunker with forty other 'persons of importance' and a large stock of essential supplies. The brave Josephus had not run away and hidden through cowardice, you must understand, but had been guided to this spider hole by 'divine providence'. Vespasian, upon hearing that this worthy foe had been located, immediately sent two tribunes 'with orders to offer Josephus safe conduct and persuade him to come out'.

Now this sounded like a decent offer to Josephus but he was suspicious that it was a trap so he declined. Another tribune was sent who happened to be an old friend of Josephus from pre-rebellion days and persuaded him that, while the ordinary soldiers were eager and capable of roasting Josephus and his friends in their cave, his 'prowess made him admired rather than hated by the generals' and that Vespasian wanted him alive not for punishment but because 'he preferred to save so excellent a man' (says Josephus). At this point Josephus, torn between surrender or death for the cause, conveniently remembered some prophetic dreams he had been sent (he was a priest as well as military commander). These had revealed to him the divine plan for chastisement of the Jews and for Vespasian's future greatness (ordained to rule the world and thus bring the kind of peace that only a global military dictatorship could). Oh yes, and these dreams also mentioned that it was Josephus' God-given task to record these events for posterity. Selflessly foregoing the opportunity of a heroic death, Josephus raised his eyes to heaven and announced:

> because Thou didst choose my spirit to make known the things to come, I yield myself willingly to the Romans that I may live, but I solemnly declare that I go not as a traitor, but as Thy servant.

Funnily enough, his forty compatriots, figuring they were in for the chastisement bit anyway, were not impressed with this decision and reminded Josephus 'how many you have persuaded to lay down their lives for liberty'. Being already resigned to die rather than submit, they made him a counter offer:

> We will lend you a sword and a hand to wield it. If you die willingly, you will die as a commander-in-chief of the Jews; if unwillingly, as a traitor.

To make their position really clear, 'they pointed their swords at him and threatened to run him through if he gave in to the Romans'. Josephus tried to reason with them. He lectured them at great length along the lines that while he obviously agreed that dying for a cause really was a great and noble thing if you really had to, the act of suicide was frowned on by God as somewhat ungrateful, what with life being His special gift and all that. This didn't wash and the angry (and probably slightly bored) mob started to close in on him, jostling and prodding at him with their swords. I'll leave it to Josephus to explain what happened next:

> In this predicament his resourcefulness did not fail him. Putting his trust in divine protection he staked his life on one last throw. 'You have chosen to die', he exclaimed; 'well then, let's draw lots and kill each other in turn. Whoever draws the first lot shall be dispatched by number two, and so on down the whole line as luck decides. In this way no one will die by his own hand [the last man presumably was to let the Romans do it] – it would be unfair when the rest were gone if one man changed his mind and saved his life.' The audience swallowed the bait, and getting his way Josephus drew lots with the rest. Without hesitation each man in turn offered his throat for the next man to cut, in the belief that a moment later his commander would die too. Life was sweet, but not so sweet as death if Josephus died with them! But Josephus – shall we put it down to divine providence or just to luck [and let's not forget the third option: cheating*] – was left with one other man. He did not relish the thought of being condemned by the lot or, if he was left till last, of staining his hand with the blood of a fellow Jew. So he used persuasion, they made a pact, and both remained alive.   [Josephus, *The Jewish War*, III.383][18]

Josephus went on to become a confidant of Vespasian and accompanied him throughout the rest of the campaign to crush his fellow Jews, leaving his completely unbiased account for posterity.

---

*Josephus being commander and priest would have administered this deadly lottery. An alternative version of his account survives, thought to be possibly his first draft, in which he does not mention divine providence or luck at this point but admits he 'counted the numbers cunningly and so managed to deceive all the others'.

Chapter 6

Soldiers' Accessories

Essential kit

Bushi hair do – The *kogai* usually carried in the sheath of a Samurai's sword doubled as a hair pin and an ear-wax remover.

Refreshingly practical design – The Galil rifle, standard issue of the Israeli military, has a beer-bottle opener built in.

Tanks brewing up – Every British tank designed from the Second World War onwards has incorporated an integral kettle for those all-important cups of tea.

Something for the weekend

In December 1943, the Germans and Russians were locked in one of the most brutal battles of the war at Stalingrad. The Germans of General von Paulus' Sixth Army had driven the defenders from almost the whole city in vicious street fighting, only to find that massive Soviet reinforcements had swept past to the north and south, cutting off their lines of supply. Reassured by Herman Goering's boasts that his air force could keep Sixth Army supplied, Hitler refused to let Paulus withdraw before he was completely encircled and ordered him to defend the recently captured ruins of Stalingrad at all costs. Paulus' troops were soon completely surrounded and cut off.

The desperate men of Sixth Army were short of winter clothing, fuel and soon ammunition. Food became so short that cases of cannibalism were rumoured. It is more than a little doubtful that Goering's overstretched air force could have kept them adequately supplied even if the airlift had been perfectly managed and executed and not hindered by terrible weather and the increasingly effective efforts of the Russian airmen. As it was, too few air supply sorties made it through to Stalingrad, and too many of these dropped their loads in Russian positions. The best the Luftwaffe managed on any particular day was still over 100 tonnes short of the amount required. Imagine then the despair of the desperate Germans of Sixth Army when they found that some of those supply containers they did manage to retrieve were full of medals and condoms.

If the shoe fits ...

In the English Civil War, each infantryman of the New Model Army was issued with three shoes, which they were intended to wear in rotation to ensure even wear. Clearly they were not shaped for either left or right foot and must have been very uncomfortable to wear. Similarly, in the early nineteenth century, US troops were also issued with shoes (but just two) which were intended to fit either foot, though in practice it meant they fit neither until well broken in. This obviously eased the logistics of resupply, but did nothing to ease the blisters of the poor soldiers.

Amazingly for a nation famous for its luxury shoe industry, Italy allowed many of her sons to fight on the icy hell of the Second World War's Eastern Front wearing boots made of cardboard.

Indian troops stationed in inaccessible Himalayan frontier posts during the border conflict with China in 1962 had to be supplied by air drops. Among many other foul-ups too numerous to list here, they found that the boots delivered for walking on the treacherous mountain slopes had no studs and their rubber soles disintegrated in the extreme cold. Nor did it greatly help that they were only supplied in sizes 6 and 12![19]

At least all these troops were given some footwear. When marines from the Roman fleet asked for an allowance for the replacement of hobnailed sandals worn out on their regular marches from Rome to the port of Ostia, the Emperor Vespasian, a notorious tightwad, ordered that they should henceforth make the march barefoot.[20]

Zulu warriors famously needed no shoes. King Shaka, the first great Zulu empire builder, instituted a training regime that included, walking over acacia thorns to toughen the feet. The impis (regiments) were made to run long distances, with the hindmost liable to being summarily stabbed to encourage the others. This worked to such a degree that a visitor to one of the battlefields of the Zulu War of 1879 found the unburied Zulu dead long-since reduced to sun-bleached skeletons, apart from the thickly calloused soles of their feet which still clung to the bone.

Rebels without a clue

During the Amercian Civil War, the Confederate states of the south, lacking the industrial base of the northern Union states, had increasing difficulties in supplying their armies with good uniforms. Even on those rare occasions when new kit was issued, it could lead to unforeseen problems.

On 14 October 1863, Confederate forces under A.P. Hill were locked in battle at Briscoe Station, when a chance arose to catch the Union II Corps at a disadvantage. Hill issued an urgent order to General Cooke's North Carolina Brigade to charge immediately. Unfortunately, the attack was delayed because Cooke's men, afraid of ruining the smart new grey jackets and blue trousers with which they had recently been issued, first took the time to change into older, battle-worn clothes. The fleeting opportunity was lost and the battle with it.[21]

Chapter 7

The Gods Are With Us

From earliest time, men have sought to find comfort amid the traumas and moral dilemmas of war by convincing themselves that their god or gods were on their side. Sometimes it is the apparent gullibility, of ancient cultures in particular, that can seem amusing to a modern, cynical eye. At others it is the realization that generals and statesmen have always been capable of cynical manipulation of beliefs and very inventive in finding loopholes in the divine will or practical workarounds.

The trouble with oracles

Before embarking upon a war the gods' advice and blessing would be sought. Whereas a sensible modern-day commander would consult intelligence reports and satellite imagery, the ancient Greeks and their neighbours would consult oracles, most notably the one at Delphi. The trouble was that their answers were notoriously ambiguous and open to interpretation. One of the earliest and most famous examples, related by Herodotus, is that of Croesus of Lydia.

Croesus already ruled wide lands in Asia Minor (modern Turkey) and was so wealthy that 'rich as Croesus' became a stock description for the very well-heeled, but he feared the rapid expansion of the neighbouring Persian empire and hit on the plan of invading them before they could invade him. Naturally he wanted the best advice so he first took steps to determine which of the many oracles was the real deal. He sent messengers out to several of the main contenders with orders to ask on a fixed date exactly what Croesus was doing back home right then. When all the answers were in, only the Delphic oracle had the right answer (stewing a lamb and a tortoise in a bronze pot).

Delighted, Croesus now attempted to grease the palm of the gods with a massive bribe which included sacrificing 3,000 each of 'every kind of appropriate animal' and sending a gift of literally tons of gold ingots, statues and cauldrons to Delphi. Finally he asked the crucial question: should he march against Persia? The oracle duly replied that 'if he attacked the Persians, he would destroy a great empire'.

Convinced that he was onto a certain winner, Croesus went ahead with his great enterprise, was beaten in battle and then captured when Cyrus of Persia launched a massive counter-invasion of Lydia. Croesus' actions had indeed led to the fall of a great empire – his own.[22]

Omens, auspices and prophecies, and how to get round them

Apart from oracles, divine hints about the outcome of a campaign or battle were thought to be given through the medium of nature – the behaviour of certain birds or animals, timely eclipses or storms could all be interpreted by those with the skill. Above all, sacrificing an animal and inspecting its innards was a favourite way of checking whether the gods approved or not. Commanders, particularly kings, sometimes performed these rituals themselves, but armies were usually accompanied by specialized priests, trained in interpreting the particular way a sheep's intestines spilled out or reading the blemishes on a cow's liver. In Greek armies such a diviner was called a *mantis* (hence the name of the praying mantis, a bug that kills its prey with surgical precision), while the Roman equivalent was the *haruspex* (literally 'gut-gazer').

Commanders also had to pay close attention to the calendar, since certain days, weeks or whole months could be declared sacred and off limits for fighting too. All these things of course could be honoured when it suited or equally often manipulated or circumvented.

Overstepping the mark

The Spartans were particularly cautious about asking for the gods' blessing before stepping over the border with an enemy state. In 494 BC, Cleomenes I was intent on indulging in a perennial favourite Spartan hobby – invading the neighbouring state of Argos.

Having advanced as far as the River Erasinus, which formed the land boundary, he offered sacrifice to the god of the river to check if it was okay to cross over. Spartan armies tramped into Argos so often he probably assumed this was a formality, but the gods were not playing ball and the omens were not at all favourable for crossing the border between their countries. 'Very well' said Cleomenes by Herodotus' account, 'I admire the god of the river for refusing to betray his countrymen. All the same, the Argives will not get away with it so lightly'. Cleomenes then marched his men to the nearest port, slipped a little bribe to the sea god Poseidon in the form of a sacrificed bull, then put his men on boats and attacked Argos from the sea instead.

Cleomenes seems to have got away with this since the gods allowed his army to win the subsequent battle with the Argives, albeit by means of another crafty ruse. The sources give two different versions of how Cleomenes gained the victory. Herodotus, our main source for the campaign, has both sides trying to be clever. As the two armies were encamped close to each other and a showdown clearly in the offing, the Argives decided to avoid being taken by surprise by ordering their men to conform to the trumpeted orders given in the Spartan camp. An elegantly simple plan: when the Spartans stood on the alert, the Argives would be ready too; when the Spartan camp was at ease, the Argives could relax. However, the canny Cleomenes soon observed what was happening and passed the word that the Spartans were to take the next signal for 'dinner's ready' to mean 'attack'. The bewildered Argives were surprised just as they'd swapped spears for spoons and were easily defeated.[23]

In Plutarch's version, Cleomenes offered the Argives a truce of seven days which they gratefully accepted. On the third night, by which time the Argives had come to trust the truce, Cleomenes attacked them under cover of darkness. When reproached for his sinful breaking of a truce, he replied that he had offered them seven days but said nothing about the nights.[24]

However victory was achieved, many of the defeated Argives escaped to seek sanctuary in a sacred wood, which the Spartans then surrounded. The Argive refugees were theoretically under divine protection amid the sacred trees (had I been a Greek ruler I would have planted my whole country with these!) but Cleomenes sent in messengers to announce to certain individuals (whose names had been provided by Argive prisoners or deserters) that their ransom had been paid by their families. As each lucky chap emerged from the woods he was seized and killed. About fifty gullible Argives had been bumped off in this way before those remaining in the woods cottoned on that something wasn't quite right. One climbed a tree and saw what was happening. So far Cleomenes had definitely been bending the rules but now, probably starting to think he could get away with anything, he definitely overstepped the mark: the sacred grove was burnt down to smoke the remainder out.

Later in the campaign, Cleomenes further tried the gods' patience when he decided to offer sacrifice at a temple to Hera, perhaps trying to get back in the divine good books. When the resident priest told the Spartan king this was not permitted, he had the priest dragged from the altar and flogged before entering the temple to perform the sacrifice himself. Cleomenes then led his army home.[25] He made it back to Sparta but the gods had the last laugh since he went insane shortly after and committed suicide in a particularly grisly way.

Date with destiny

In 419 BC, the army of Argos in Greece invaded the territory of the neighbouring city-state of Epidaurus twice. On the first occasion they began their expedition four days before the onset of the month of Carneus, which was sacred and precluded such activity. Fully intending to take more than four days over the campaign, the Argive leadership attempted to get round the time constraint by simply altering their calendar and declaring that each day was still the fourth day before Carneus. When the Epidaurans called upon their allies for assistance they refused to break the ban on making war during Carneus, so Epidaurus stood alone as the Argives started laying waste to her territory.

Eventually the other nearby Greek states did decide the Argives were being just too cheeky. In a fit of well-intentioned half-measure taking of which the UN would have been proud, they held a conference at which it was decided to send envoys to prevent a pitched battle taking place. The Argive army withdrew for a while then simply resumed their attack once the envoys had gone home. The Spartans now sent an army to aid the Epidaurans but the omens taken as the border was about to be crossed were not favourable so they went home again. The Argives went on their merry, destructive way during which, according to the historian Thucydides, they 'laid waste about a third of the territory of Epidaurus and then returned home'.[26]

A similar incident occurred early in Alexander the Great's invasion of the Persian Empire in 334 BC. Shortly before the Battle of the Granicus River, Alexander was reminded that the month of Artemisius had given way to that of Daesius, during which no Macedonian king ever made war. Alexander responded by simply declaring that they would call it a second Artemisius – you could get away with that sort of thing if you were descended from Herculles on one side and Achilles on the other (it doesn't work on book editors who are chasing overdue manuscripts).

If at first you don't succeed ...

The day of an actual battle was a prime time for sacrificing and taking omens. While the armies were drawing up their battle lines, generals and priests could always find the time to open up a sheep or two to check that the gods were onside. And if the fickle gods did not give the right answer at the first time of asking, then you simply brought up another poor dumb animal and tried again. A great example of this is at the Battle of Plataea in northern Greece in 479 BC. The two armies faced each other across the little stream of the Asopus for a full ten days because neither side could get omens favourable for giving battle. Each day the troops would deploy in their battle lines and the diviners would perform their gory rituals but the Olympians were not having any of it; this despite both sides having prepared for the campaign season by signing up a celebrity diviner for their team. The Spartans had even granted theirs the coveted Spartan citizenship while the invading Persians, playing an away game (and their own monotheistic religion not withstanding), had employed a Greek who would obviously know how to approach the local gods.

On the eleventh day, Xerxes decided to throw caution to the wind and attack anyway. The Persians, who had many archers, approached to easy bow range, set up a barricade of propped-up shields and began peppering their Spartan enemies with showers of arrows. The Spartans, having no long-range weapons but being hard as nails in close combat, clearly needed to get to grips with the Persians as soon as possible. Yet, before he could order a counter-attack, King Pausanius had to check the omens. An animal was duly disembowelled but something in its icky bits told the officiating priest the gods did not favour an assault. As Spartan bodies stuck with Persian arrows started hitting the dirt around him, Pausanius calmly ordered another sacrifice. This was still in progress when one unit took the initiative and charged the Persians. Lo and behold! The omens suddenly came out right and Pausanius ordered the rest of his Spartans to follow. The Persians were defeated and Greece saved.[27]

But the prize for sheer persistence has to go to the Roman consul Aemilius Paulus before the Battle of Pydna. On the night before the battle, the Romans and their Macedonian enemies were encamped close together, preparing for the expected showdown. That night can be exactly dated as 22 June 168 BC because there was a lunar eclipse. Although the cleverest Greek thinkers had long understood the actual cause of such phenomena, they were still generally taken as powerful omens. According to Plutarch the Macedonians were downcast as they read it as a portent of the eclipse of a king – and as the republican Romans did not have kings this left their own King Perseus clearly in Fate's firing line. In the other camp, Plutarch tells us that when they saw the moon disappearing the Romans 'according to their custom, tried to call her light back by the clashing of

---

* The diviner used by the Persians was a chap called Hegistratus of Elis who had a score to settle. He had previously been arrested and sentenced to death in Sparta for reasons now unknown but staged a remarkable escape. While awaiting execution he was secured by one foot but had somehow smuggled in a knife with which he cut away just enough of his own foot to escape. He then managed to break a hole through his cell wall and escaped cross-country to a city hostile to Sparta, where he had a wooden replacement part made for his mutilated foot.

bronze utensils and by holding up many blazing fire-brands and torches towards the heavens'. Plutarch tells us that Aemilius Paulus himself had some knowledge of the science of eclipses but he decided to play it safe by sacrificing eleven heifers to the moon to thank her for her return.

At dawn, as the Roman camp clamoured with preparation for the expected battle, Paulus sacrificed an ox to Hercules. The omens were not favourable so another ox was prepared and the ritual started over again. Again the lay of the intestines, the shape of the liver or the flow of the blood was not quite right and Paulus would not order the army out into battle array – another ox and again the same thing. While his officers champed at the bit, Paulus insisted on getting it right. Another ox and still the gods would not give the nod. Noon came and went and still it went on with ox after ox. It was late afternoon before the twenty-first beast finally produced the desired result and the legions were ordered to deploy. The battle proved to be worth the wait since the fighting was all over in the hour and the Romans won a famous victory.[28]

Don't take no for an answer

In 388 BC, King Agesipolis was intent on outdoing the exploits of his colleague (the Spartans had two kings at a time, usually one went off to war while the other was kept at home as a spare). He was preparing to invade Argos at the first sign of spring and determined not to be easily put off. The sacrifices at the border went well so the Spartans stepped over and began laying waste to the enemy farmland in time-honoured fashion. They had not got far, however, when two Argive priests turned up wearing festive garlands on their heads. These complained to Agesipolis that Argos was currently celebrating a holy month and that a sacred truce should therefore be observed. This was apparently the first the Argives had mentioned about this convenient festival and Agesipolis thought he could smell a rat. Indeed, he had expected just such a trick and had taken the precaution of consulting not one but two oracles on the matter prior to the invasion. Both had reassured him that he need not accept or honour a truce made in bad faith. The enemy priests were sent packing and the Spartans continued their march undeterred.

As Agesipolis and his entourage settled down to a well-earned meal on that first evening of the invasion, the libations to the gods had just been poured when the earth shook beneath them. Knowing the drill for earthquakes, the whole Spartan army immediately sang a hymn to Poseidon. The shaking stopped but the men, remembering a previous occasion when such a tremor had caused Agesipolis to postpone an invasion, started making ready to head for home forthwith. Agesipolis quickly pointed out that on that previous occasion Poseidon had sent the earthquake before he had entered enemy territory, a clear sign that he forbade the invasion. This time, however, the god had sent his sign once they had already crossed the border, which was obviously completely different and should be interpreted as a definite thumbs-up for the enterprise.

Having taken the trouble to find out from veterans in the ranks how far a recent invasion under his co-king had gone, Agesipolis went one better by leading the army right up to within bowshot of the city of Argos itself. Here some enemy cavalrymen, locked out by their terrified compatriots within as they hurriedly shut the gates, 'had to cling to the wall, spread-eagled under the battlements like bats'. All was going well and Agesipolis' decision to press on seemed vindicated. However, when the army settled down to spend the night near the city 'a thunderbolt fell in the camp, killing some men directly and some from the shock'. Even this clear hint had no immediate effect upon the thick-skinned Spartan king, though doubtless there must have been some jitters among the rank and file. Agesipolis hit on the plan of building a permanent fort in Argive territory, covering the passes into Lakonia, and consulted the omens. It was only when several animals had been sacrificed and the livers of all the victims found to be seriously deformed ('without lobes') that Agesipolis finally decided he had pushed his luck far enough and led the army home.[29]

Playing chicken with the gods

Although the Romans often seem to be a supremely practical people, especially in military matters, they could be every bit as superstitious as the Greeks and their commanders defied the will of the gods at their peril.

In 249 BC, a Roman fleet of 120 ships commanded by the consul Publius Appius Pulcher spotted the vessels of the enemy. Pulcher ordered the attack to be sounded. An attendant priest pointed out that the sacred chickens, who had perhaps noticed that the Carthaginian fleet was superior, were not eating their corn and that this was not a good omen. Pulcher, determined not to be deprived of his shot at glory, angrily hurled the chickens overboard with the witty rejoinder: 'If they won't eat, they can drink instead!' He then sailed on to a crushing defeat, the crews of ninety-three of his ships soon joining the chickens in their unscheduled swim.

The ritual self-sacrifice of Decius Mus (341 BC and 295 BC)

In 341 BC the Romans fell out with their Latin allies and their respective armies squared up to each other at Veseris, near Mount Vesuvius, the following year. As the Latins usually fought alongside the Romans using the same organization and tactics, the two Roman consuls in command knew they were in for a particularly tough day at the office. Indeed it was the discipline and self sacrifice of these two men, Titus Manlius and Publius Decimus Mus, which was to make the difference between the evenly matched opponents.

In the run up to the battle, the son of Titus Manlius, also called Titus Manlius, was serving in the army with the cavalry as any young aristocrat should and was out on patrol when he was challenged by a Latin horseman to single combat. Manlius junior could not resist, thinking to impress his father who had himself won fame for killing an enemy champion in a similar duel years before (and proudly bore the nickname 'Torquatus' after the gold torc he took from the corpse as a trophy). Young Manlius won the fight, stripped the Latin warrior of his weapons and armour and took them back to show daddy. Old Torquatus, while duly proud of his boy's prowess, pointed out that he had broken his standing consular order against engaging the enemy without consent. The punishment for such an offence was death and, to make the supreme example to the rest of the army, he had his son bound and beheaded on the spot. The legions were thus left in no doubt that their commanders meant business and would demand absolute discipline and obedience on the day of battle. Then it would be the turn of the other consul to make a sacrifice for the greater good (though I leave it to any father reading this to judge which sacrifice was the greater).

The night before battle, so the story goes, both consuls had been visited in their dreams by the apparition of 'a man of superhuman stature and majesty'. This god, for such he surely was, told them that the general of one side in the coming battle, and the army of the other, were due as an offering to the gods of the Underworld and to Mother Earth. If the general of either army was prepared to offer himself up to death in the coming battle, the gods would take him and the enemy's legions as their due. Finding they'd had the same creepy dream, the consuls ordered sacrifices to the gods and, when the officiating gut-gazer's pronouncements seemed to concur, they made a plan. First, the deal offered by the apparition was immediately announced to the assembled army so that they would not be demoralized by the loss of a consul in the fighting. Then the two, who would each command one half of the army, agreed that they would commence battle as normal, but if any part of the Roman battle line started to give way, then the respective consul would do the necessary deed.

When the battle finally got underway, it turned out to be on the left wing, where Decimus Mus commanded, that things first started to go against the Romans, their first line being pushed back onto their reserves. As the Latins continued to surge forward, Decius asked a priest stationed nearby for the purpose to quickly run him through the proper rituals for *devotio*, dedication to the gods. This, in case you want to try it, involved donning his best purple-edged toga, veiling his head, touching his chin with one hand while standing on a spear and beseeching a long list of gods to afflict the enemy with terror, dread and death. Ending with the words 'I devote myself and with me the legions and auxiliaries of our enemies to the gods of the Underworld and to Earth', he sent a message to his colleague saying what he'd done.

Finally, hitching up his toga, Decimus Mus took up his weapons, vaulted onto his horse and spurred it straight towards the enemy battle line. The sudden assault of this obvious madman hurtling towards them threw the advancing Latins into some confusion. Decimus penetrated deep into their formation 'as men shrank away as before some death-dealing star' before finally being brought down by a rain of javelins. His example put fresh courage into the wavering Roman troops who, inspired by a thirst for revenge and the belief that the enemy were now doomed to defeat, went on to rout the enemy 'with such slaughter that they left scarcely a quarter of their opponents alive'.

The consul's self sacrifice made an impression on nobody more than his own son, also called Publius Decius Mus.* So much so that in 295 BC, when he was himself consul and a battle against the Gauls seemed lost, he repeated his father's trick and rode to his death amid the enemy ranks. The Gauls immediately around Decius' corpse were allegedly overcome with a kind of shock so that they 'kept throwing their javelins without aim or purpose, as if they had lost their wits, while some of them were stupefied and could think neither of fighting nor flight'. By contrast, the Roman soldiers, who had actually been fleeing, were inspired to return to the fight and won the day.

UFO halts ancient battle

Many of the phenomena interpeted by the ancients as signs from the gods are easy to laugh off as superstitious minds reading meaning into perfectly normal natural occurrences, like eclipses and lightning strikes. But what are we to make of the following?:

In 73 BC, a Roman army under the consul Lucullus was invading the territory of Mithridates VI of Pontus, when its path was blocked by a Pontic army on an open plain in Bithynia (in modern Turkey). Both armies had deployed for battle and the action was set to kick off at any moment when, in broad daylight under the eyes of about 60,000 men, this happened:

> as they were on the point of joining battle, with no apparent change of weather, but all on a sudden, the sky burst asunder, and a huge, flame-like body was seen to fall between the two armies. In shape it was most like a wine jar, and in colour, like molten silver. [Plutarch, *Lucullus*, 8][30]

---

*Originality wasn't a major priority in naming Roman babies, or Greek ones for that matter. The current trend of inventing new personal names out of random syllables or adding a letter to an existing one would have been abhorrent to any parent in the Classical world (I mean, Kian? Really?).

Deciding the gods were clearly trying to say something but unsure what, both armies withdrew to a safe distance and battle was averted.

God's little helpers?

Herodotus tells the fantastic tale of an army laid low by divine intervention. As the Assyrian King Senacherib was approaching Egypt with a large army of invasion, the current pharaoh, who had made himself very unpopular with the warrior class, was dismayed to find that his soldiers all refused to take up arms. Making a beeline for a temple he prayed for guidance at the feet of a statue until he fell asleep. He had a dream (a favourite method of communication for the ancient gods) in which he was told not to lose heart, for if he marched boldly out to meet the enemy army, 'the god himself would send him helpers'.

Trusting in divine providence, the pharaoh hastily gathered an army of 'shopkeepers, artisans and market people', the soldiers of course still being on strike, and marched to Pelusium, blocking the route the invaders must take. On the eve of the expected battle, with the two armies camped close to each other, the pharaoh's faith was rewarded:

> As he lay here facing the enemy, thousands of field-mice swarmed over the Assyrians during the night, and ate their quivers, their bowstrings, and the leather handles of their shields, so that on the following day, having no arms to fight with, they abandoned their position and suffered severe losses during the retreat. [Herodotus II.141]

In this sign conquer

Ah, I know what you are thinking: those silly superstitious pagans – fancy believing in omens and believing they could summon divine aid in battle through arcane rituals. Well, consider the incident that directly led to Christianity being elevated from a minority cult for women, dropouts and slaves, to one of the world's dominant religions.

In 312, the Roman Empire was in the final throes of a vicious and bloody civil war. Constantine, having ruthlessly done away with most of his rivals for power, was approaching Rome from the north. He knew his opponent, Maxentius, had a massive numerical advantage, with perhaps twice as many men. At this stage Constantine was a pagan but his mother was a Christian. Apparently he decided to give the Christian god a chance to show what he could do and prayed for a sign to guide him. According to the historian Eusebius, who claimed to have got it from Constantine himself, his sign soon appeared:

> About the time of the midday sun, when day was just turning, he said he saw with his own eyes, up in the sky and resting over the sun, a cross-shaped trophy formed from light, and a text attached to it that said 'by this conquer'.[31]

Conveniently, Constantine was not actually with the main body of his army when he saw this, but off with a detachment of loyal guards. In any case, he did not immediately get the meaning of this sign but meditated upon it until it grew dark and he fell asleep. A giant sign in the sky obviously having been too subtle, God then sent Christ to appear to him in a dream, again showed him the sign 'and urged him to make himself a copy of the sign which had appeared in the sky, and to use this as protection against the attacks of the enemy'.[32] On waking, Constantine finally knew what to do and in suspiciously short order had a banner made by some jewellers and goldsmiths who were fortunately found nearby. It took the form of a gold-plated cross topped by a monogram formed of the Greek letters chi and rho (looking like an X laid over a P), these being the first two letters of 'Christ'.

With the banner made and the army assured that divine providence would help them overcome the enemy's superior numbers, Constantine and his troops continued their march on Rome. North of the Tiber they found Maxentius' host waiting for them, deployed with its back to the river. What followed is known as the Battle of the Milvian Bridge. Attacking with the magic banner in the vanguard, it was obviously divine assistance that ensured an early success was turned to a complete victory when the single pontoon bridge over the river miraculously collapsed under the weight of thousands of Maxentius' heavily-armoured retreating troops. Maxentius himself was among the thousands drowned and Constantine found himself the undisputed ruler of the empire. In gratitude he converted to Christianity and effectively raised it to the official state religion. Christianity of course was far less tolerant than paganism had been. The Church bloodily and systematically suppressed paganism and the rest is history; the blood-soaked history of sectarian violence in the name of a supposedly benevolent and forgiving god.

Good medicine and fetishes

Of course, where Christianity had not spread its tentacles, warriors continued to cling to the silly, superstitious old ways, looking to magic symbols and charms for protection in battle. As late as the nineteenth century, Native American braves daubed themselves and their horses with spots representing hailstones which were thought to be powerful 'medicine' against bullets. On the other side of the Atlantic in West Africa, the fierce Ashante warriors of what is now Ghana went into battle with magic charms or 'fetishes' sewn into their robes to ward off harm. Neither paint nor trinkets actually protected any of the thousands who were bravely mown down by the modern rifles and machine guns of the US Cavalry or British 'Redcoats'. Serves them right for being so naive and gullible right? The millions of St Christopher medallions and crucifixes that have been worn and kissed for good luck by Christian Tommies and GIs through the carnage of two world wars and up to the present are completely different of course, though they just as frequently end up as grave goods.

Chapter 8

An Army Marches on its Stomach (and its Liver)

Soldiers being soldiers (actually, soldiers generally being men), like few things more than a drink and a good meal, but these basic human needs have often proved a weakness.

Honey, I doped the army

In 401 BC, a large group of Greek mercenaries found itself cut off in the heart of the Persian Empire when the rebel they were working for was killed. Their senior officers were treacherously murdered while trying to explain to the Persian king that it was nothing personal, just business. Electing new officers, including an Athenian called Xenophon who by all accounts was a military genius (actually, his own account is really the only one we have, so that figures), they made an epic march through hundreds of miles of hostile territory, beating off attacks by Persian armies and local tribesmen. During this famous 'March of the Ten Thousand', Xenophon records how the hungry Greeks, having just chased off some local tribesmen, were delighted to find their villages contained a large number of beehives full of delicious honey. Unfortunately, thanks to a particular kind of rhododendron frequented by the local bees, it was potent stuff:

> all the soldiers who ate the honey went off their heads and suffered from vomiting and diarrhoea and were unable to stand upright. Those who had only eaten a little behaved as though they were drunk, and those who had eaten a lot were like mad people. Some actually died. So there were numbers of them lying on the ground, as though after a defeat, and there was a general state of despondency.   [Xenophon, *Anabasis*, IV.8]

Apparently it was a full twenty-four hours before the army was all conscious again (apart from those that died, obviously) and not until the third and fourth days that 'they were able to get up and felt just as though they had been taking medicine'. Three days' march lost to one honey of a hangover!

Rebels get absolutely slaughtered

When Maharbal was sent to crush the rebellion of some of Carthage's African subjects, he capitalized on their known fondness of wine. After an inconclusive skirmish the rebels were pleased to find that the Carthaginians had withdrawn. What is more, they appeared to have made off in real haste since they had left some of their baggage, including a good quantity of wine, behind in their abandoned camp. A victory party was soon in full swing, 'in a frenzy of delight' according to Frontinus, but what the revellers didn't know was that the wily Maharbal had spiked the drink with 'mandragora, which in potency is somewhere between a poison and a soporific'. It may have made the party go with a bit of an extra swing for a while, since a little mandragora, or mandrake as it is better known, causes hallucinations and delirium. Take a little more, however, and it causes unconsciousness and even coma. The Carthaginians returned a little later and 'either made them prisoner or slaughtered them while they lay stretched out as if dead'.[33]

Raising the steaks ...

Frontinus' book *Stratagems* contains two variations on Maharbal's trick. The Carthaginian genius, Hannibal (he of elephant fame) noted that both his own army and that of his Roman foes had encamped in a region where there were few trees to provide firewood. This was a problem in the days before ready rations and self-heating tins but he decided to turn it to his advantage. He marched his army away as if retiring from the enemy, in his apparent haste leaving many cattle behind in his abandoned camp. When the Romans took possession of the camp they happily set upon this windfall of fresh meat. Frontinus reports they 'gorged themselves with flesh, which, owing to the scarcity of firewood, was raw and indigestible'. All that remained was for Hannibal to march back during the night and attack them while they were still trying to sleep off their indigestion, inflicting severe casualties.

The Roman general Tiberius Gracchus played a similarly deadly prank when he learnt that the enemy army were suffering from lack of provisions. He abandoned his camp, leaving it stuffed with 'eatables of all kinds'. The ravenous enemy duly occupied the camp and started stuffing themselves silly with all the goodies they could find. The Romans then returned with the now-familiar result.[34]

A rum deal for the Kaiser

In March 1918 the British achieved a similar effect to Gracchus' trick by complete accident. The German Spring Offensive finally broke the long 'trenchlock' of the Western Front, using superior tactics (with a lot of help from the fog) to send the British Fifth Army reeling back in retreat and prompting Haig's famous 'backs to the wall' order (the fact that his back was to the wall of a cushy chateau rather than the slimy side of a trench is irrelevant; it was a damned stirring speech and captures the desperation of the situation).

The Germans, who, thanks to the Royal Navy's blockade, had long since been reduced to a diet of ersatz coffee (made from acorns and coal tar) and other substitute foods (e.g. rice shaped to resemble lamb chops, complete with a 'bone' made of wood) overran British positions stuffed with chocolate and other luxuries sent from loving relatives, in addition to the official rum ration and liberal helpings of French wine. Besides the psychological effect of realizing the Tommies had been having it relatively easy, the attack started to run out of steam as the German soldiers set about the booze and chocolate like Grandma at Christmas. One German officer reported seeing 'the streets running with wine'. They were in no position to resist effectively when the British got their act together again and led the sustained counterattacks that eventually forced the German into unconditional surrender (ably supported by the gallant French and the Americans who had finally joined the party).

Not-so-sweet success

In 634 Khalid ibn Walid, also known as 'the Sword of Allah', achieved a major strategic surprise over the Byzantine enemy by marching from Iraq to Syria directly across the inhospitable Syrian desert. There was an oasis a couple of days in, but then many days further to travel without further fresh water. There was no way his camel-mounted forced could carry enough water for so many men and beasts to make the crossing, but Khalid had a cunning plan. They marched the first two-day stage to an oasis, the last fresh water before Syria, without a drop to drink. The camels, now very thirsty, needed little encouragement to fill their bellies with water. Khalid then had his men bind their mouths shut to prevent them eating or chewing the cud and proceeded on the main part of the crossing. The camels, adapted to retain water in their bodies, had effectively become walking flasks. At intervals, some of the beasts would be slain and their stomachs cut open so Khalid's men could drink the water stored within. Warm and sour with digestive juices as it must have been, it kept them alive and, arriving by such an unexpected route, they took the Byzantine forces in the rear and defeated them.

One for the road – the Battle of Karansebes

In 1788, Emperor Joseph II of Austria was hell-bent on driving the Turks out of Transylvania (yes, it really exists; it's now part of Romania). He gathered an impressive army of 172,000 men drawn from the many ethnic groups under his rule, though a fifth of these were lost before the invasion even got going, having encamped in a well-known malaria hotspot near Belgrade. Undeterred, when Joseph heard that a Turkish army was marching out to forestall his invasion, he reacted by advancing with just half his remaining force, about 70,000 men, to seek out the enemy and give battle.

Towards the end of a long day of marching, the leading elements of the army reached the town of Karansebes, crossing a bridge over the River Timis. The Hussar units who were scouting ahead soon came across some gypsies who had barrels of booze to sell, probably the local schnapps. The Hussars were soon having a high old time and as the first infantry units started to arrive, thirsty and having probably been eating the dust kicked up by the Hussars all day, they tried to get a piece of the action. The Hussars, however, were not of a mind to share with footslogging riff raff and let them know in no uncertain terms that they were not invited to this party. An altercation broke out. Shots were fired and someone, shouted *Turci! Turci*! (The Turks! The Turks!), possibly in jest or to scare the Hussars. The drunken Hussars, thinking the enemy really were upon them, galloped back the way they had come to save themselves and raise the alarm. The sound of shots and wild horsemen thundering towards them out of the gathering darkness threw the rest of the army into a panic. Some started firing wildly into the shadows, while others tried to turn back and re-cross the bridge to put the river between themselves and the Turks. This, of course, caused pandemonium as the main column was still trying to cross. Many men ended up in the river, the frail Emperor Joseph himself being tipped out of his carriage into the water.

Command and control in the Austrian army was always something of a problem as the various contingents all spoke different languages and could not understand each other. At night and with every man fearing they'd been ambushed by the whole Turkish army, it was even worse. By the time the emperor had dragged himself ashore and mounted a horse to try to restore order, absolute chaos reigned with infantry and even artillery firing furiously at anything that moved. By morning the army had retreated, leaving around 10,000 dead and wounded on the field. The Turks were still two days' march away.

Bitter taste of defeat

In the First World War, Major T.E. Lawrence (better known as Lawrence of Arabia) was one of several officers sent by the British to support the Arab revolt against their Turkish overlords, who were allied to the Germans and threatened British interests in Egypt and India.

By making promises of British gold and weapons (which were more or less fulfilled) and guarantees of Arab independence after the war (not so much), Lawrence helped induce the fractious Bedouin tribes to join the revolt under the leadership of Faisal bin Hussein bin Ali al-Hashemi, a descendant of the Prophet Mohammed. But, as the Arabs' favourite pastime had until recently been stealing each other's camels and women and killing each other in endless clan feuds over stolen camels and women and killings, the alliance was still a fragile thing when their forces tried to make a stand near Nakhl Mubarak to delay the Turkish advance on the vital port of Yenbo in December 1916.

The battle had been proceeding well for Faisal's forces, despite their two British-supplied artillery pieces being worn-out relics of the Boer War with 'no sights, nor range-finders, no range tables, no high explosive'. As evening approached, Faisal was beginning to entertain hopes of a clear victory but the Juheina tribal contingent securing his left flank suddenly stopped fighting and withdrew to their camping ground in the rear. Fearing the worst, Faisal ordered his whole force to make a rapid retreat, riding through the night to reach Yenbo, where Lawrence was busy readying the town's defences.

Faisal was just recounting these events to Lawrence and the two of them were cursing the treachery of the Juheina, when Abd el Kerim, emir of the Juheina burst in, kissed Faisal's headrope in respectful greeting and sat down beside them. When Faisal asked what he thought was doing there, he expressed his dismay at being suddenly abandoned by Faisal and the rest of the army as he and his men had just fought the Turks alone all through the night and without artillery support, before eventually being forced to withdraw. A perplexed Faisal explained that he had only withdrawn when he saw the Juheina were abandoning him and asked why they had, at the climax of the battle, retired to their tents. Abd el Kerim replied 'Only to make ourselves a cup of coffee'.[35]

Desecrated vegetables

Though the northern states generally enjoyed a massive advantage in the American Civil War due to being more industrially advanced, some of the products of modern manufacturing techniques were better than others. The problem of feeding the unprecedented number of soldiers was solved in part by modern preservation techniques and mass production. Union soldiers were sometimes sent blocks of desiccated vegetables, but a trooper of the 3rd Iowa Cavalry Regiment described how these were received:

> [They] also sent us compressed cakes which Lun, our mess cook, calls 'desecrated vegetables'. We have boiled, baked, fried, stewed, pickled, sweetened, salted it, and tried it in puddings, cakes and pies; but it sets all modes of cooking at defiance, so the boys break it up and smoke it in their pipes!

Chapter 9

Unlikely Survivors

Reading accounts of wars and battles through the ages, one can only conclude that the Grim Reaper himself finds it all a bit confusing and plies his trade with a frankly disappointing disregard for any systematic appraisal of the situation. While millions of soldiers who are doing their best to survive are cut down, often by stray missiles not even aimed at them, others repeatedly thumb their noses at Death and yet walk away from situations that should by rights have finished them off.

Alexander the Great chancer

Possibly the most famous man renowned for cheating death was Alexander the Great. Considered among the greatest generals of all time, the young Macedonian king led his army on a continuous thirteen-year conquering spree that left him with an empire stretching from the Libyan Desert in the west to Afghanistan and northern India in the east. And when I say he led them, I mean he really led them from the very front. His trademark battle-winning tactic was a cavalry charge into the enemy lines with him riding at the point of a wedge formation and in sieges he was not averse to leading the storming parties up a ladder or through a breach in the wall. Inevitably, then, he had his share of knocks and close calls with death:

Battle of Granicus, 334 BC – Leading a cavalry charge across a river defended by Persian cavalry, Alexander has his helmet split by a sword blow which nicks his scalp. He then leads another charge on the enemy's reserve of Greek mercenary spearmen. Charging on horseback against fresh heavy infantry, especially spearmen, has always been near the top of the things-not-to-do-in-battle list and Alexander has his horse killed beneath him by a sword thrust through its ribs. The Greeks, however, are cut to pieces.

Battle of Issus, 333 BC – Another all-out charge across a defended river, this time against enemy infantry. Alexander is stabbed in the thigh but gallops on to another glorious victory.

Siege of Tyre, 332 BC – Leading a picked force to punish mountain tribesmen, Alexander and a few companions become separated from the main force and, as night falls, find themselves surrounded by the campfires of the enemy. Alexander sneaks off to the nearest enemy outpost, kills two men with his dagger and takes a fiery brand back to build his own fire. When angry tribesmen find and attack the intrepid band, Alexander kills several and sees them off, safely rejoining his army next day. Later, he personally leads the storming party that finally breaks into Tyre.

Siege of Gaza, 332 BC – Alexander is hit by a missile hurled by a siege catapult which pierces his shield, his armour and his shoulder. He continues to direct operations and the city is eventually taken amid great slaughter.

Battle of Gaugamela, 331 BC – Attacking an army at least three times the size of his own, Alexander leads another decisive charge, carving his way through the Persian royal guard and chasing off their king. His Royal Squadron are then attacked by masses of enemy cavalry. Heavily outnumbered, Alexander reacts as any good psychopath should and rides right at the foremost Persian, skewering him. Although he emerges from the ensuing scrap unscathed, sixty of his companions are killed around him before the enemy quit the field.

Afghanistan, 329 BC – Alexander leads a gruelling march across 75 miles of waterless desert. When a river is finally reached, many of his men die after drinking too rapidly from its icy waters. Later, during a skirmish with hostile tribesmen, Alexander takes an arrow to the leg which damages the fibula.

River Jaxartes, 329 BC – Attempting to storm a fortified town, Alexander is struck on the neck by a rock dropped from the walls and thought dead. Recovering consciousness he resumes command of the siege despite concussion, blurred vision and impaired speech. He is still unable to speak properly and has bone fragments working their way out of his earlier leg wound when he leads a successful expedition across the Jaxartes (Syr Daryu) and defeats the hitherto-invincible Scythians.

The relief of Maracanda, 329 BC – Shortly after defeating the Scythians, and despite being laid low by a bout of dysentery, Alexander quits his sickbed to lead a forced march of over 150 miles in three days and nights to relieve the besieged garrison of Maracanda.

Sogdiana, winter 329/8 BC – Crossing mountains, Alexander survives a sudden ice storm in which the temperature drops so rapidly and so far below zero that many of his men are frozen to death like statues in animated poses.

Battle of the Hydaspes River, 326 BC – In a battle which saw Alexander's cavalry faced by elephants for the first time, he himself emerges unscathed, despite being in the thick of it as usual, but his famous horse, Bucephalus, receives wounds that shortly prove fatal.

'The town of the Mallians', India, 326 BC – Alexander's guardsmen have already stormed the outer defences when Alexander decides they are being too hesitant in assaulting the walls of the inner citadel. In fact their reluctance is partly caused by insufficient scaling ladders but Alexander has no time for such excuses. Seizing one of the few ladders available, he places it and is the first up onto the wall. His shamed and inspired men surge forward to join him but the ladder breaks, leaving their king isolated atop the wall and targeted by missiles from a mass of enemies inside. Alexander leaps down into the midst of the defenders, killing several with his sword. The Mallians back off and bombard Alexander with missiles; an 'arrow two cubits long' pierces his breastplate and enters his right lung, knocking him to the ground. Thinking the king done for, the archer approaches to strip him of his magnificent armour, but Alexander manages to get to his knees and kill him with his sword. Remaining defiant as his strength, and much of his blood, drains from him, according to one ancient account he even makes a *Matrix*-style beckoning gesture to the enemy to bring it on.[36] As he finally collapses and the enemy close in, three of Alexander's personal bodyguard reach and stand over him. One of this trio is killed and the others seriously wounded before more reinforcements arrive, the men having formed human ladders and torn gates from their hinges in their desperation to get over or through the wall to save their beloved king.

A barbed arrow has to be cut from Alexander's chest with much loss of blood. Although his wound is very serious, after a week or so he manages to mount his horse to parade himself before his troops to prove he still lives.

Back to Babylon, 325 BC – Returning from his conquests Alexander sends part of his army back by sea while he leads the rest on an unnecessary march through the Gedrosian Desert, just to prove he can really. Thirst and heat exhaustion deliver thousands of the Macedonians into Death's bony clutches but Alexander, sharing his men's hardships despite being barely recuperated from his chest wound (famously refusing to drink until there was enough water for all), eludes him once more.

Alexander finally died in his bed in Babylon in 323 BC at the age of thirty-three. Speculation still surrounds the exact cause but one recent theory is an accidental overdose of drugs taken to relieve the pains of his many old war wounds.

Romans with real bite

Book VII of Pliny's *Natural History*, which reads a bit like an ancient Roman *Guinness Book of Records*, singles out two men (both Romans of course) as remarkable exemplars of 'valour and fortitude'. The first was Licinius Siccius, also known as 'Dentatus', which literally means 'him with the teeth'. This could be a comment on his ferocity, but given the Roman penchant for nasty nicknames probably meant goofy or buck-toothed. Anyway, this toothy warrior served Rome in the early days of the Republic, shortly after the expulsion of their last king around 510 BC. He apparently fought in 120 battles and won 8 single combats (i.e. the one-on-one duels that often took place before the armies set about each other in earnest). He stripped the armour of thirty-four enemies as trophies, (taking the armour of those slain as trophies, particularly that of officers, was an honourable deed back then, now it would be 'looting') and was awarded scores of decorations for valour by his grateful commanders, including fourteen civic crowns for rescuing fellow Romans in mortal peril and three mural crowns for being the first over the walls of an enemy city. In the process he picked up 'the glorious marks of forty-five scars and never a one in the back parts of his body' (i.e. none received in the back while running away).

Impressive stuff, but Pliny reserves his highest praise for Marcus Sergius who went above and beyond the call of duty in the late third century BC. In only his second action Sergius lost his right hand. He fought four more battles 'with his left hand only', including one in which he had two horses killed under him, before having a new right hand made of iron. Thus re-armed, he went on to serve in many more campaigns, being wounded at least another twenty-three times. He was twice captured by Hannibal, once being kept in chains for twenty months, but both times escaped to return to duty. His final reward for this exceptional devotion was to be barred from attending certain rites and sacrifices because of his disfiguring wounds and missing hand.

In your face, Romans

When the great East Roman general Belisarius was defending Rome against the Goths in 537, two members of his guard received injuries that warranted detailed mention by the contemporary historian, Procopius. During one Gothic attack, a guard named Cutilas, a Thracian by origin, was impaled by a javelin in his skull yet continued to fight on until the Goths were repulsed. It was only when army doctors later removed the javelin that the excessive force required caused more damage and he died. Perhaps they should have left it in there; he would have had trouble wearing hats or getting through doorways, but you can't have everything.

One of his colleagues, Arzes, was luckier when he was hit in the face by an arrow which penetrated deep between his right eye and his nose. The Goths used arrowheads with backward-pointing barbs so the arrow could not be withdrawn the way it had entered without causing massive damage. Fortunately, one of the army physicians gave Arzes a thorough examination and found a lump under the skin on the back of his head. A quick incision confirmed this to be the tip of the offending arrow. The feathered end was therefore cut off in front and the business end pulled through from the back. Arzes apparently survived with hardly a scar.[37]

Extreme courage is standard for British redcoats

Throughout history, military units have attached great significance to various flags, banners and standards. They have a symbolic value way beyond their practical function of marking a unit's position on the battlefield. Embodying the collective spirit of the men who served under them, they were objects of great pride and their loss in battle was the worst disgrace and a severe blow to morale. Nowhere was this more true than in the British army of the eighteenth and nineteenth centuries, when each battalion would carry two flags, or 'colours', into battle, one being the King's (or Queen's) colour, consisting of the Union Flag, and the other being the unit-specific regimental colour. As the following examples demonstrate, the men who bore the colours were quite prepared to die to protect them but, remarkably, neither of these two did.

Ensign Latham at Albuera

At the Battle of Albuera in Spain, on 17 May 1811, a command blunder left the British 3rd Foot (East Kent) Regiment, the famous Buffs, isolated and attacked on all sides by French cavalry. As the horsemen closed in for the kill, Ensign Thomas, bearing the regimental colour was soon killed and the flag captured, but Lieutenant Matthew Latham, bearing the King's colour, proved a tougher proposition.

A French hussar grabbed the flagstaff with one hand and aimed a blow with his sabre at Latham's head, which sliced off his nose and half his face. Undeterred, Latham kept his grip on the pole, while apparently crying 'I shall surrender it only with my life'. Another Hussar then severed his left arm, the one holding the flag, briefly freeing it from its stubborn guardian. This, also, Latham shrugged off; throwing away his sword, he grabbed the flagstaff with his right hand and resumed the lethal tug of war with the hussars, who were now joined also by some of Napoleon's famous Polish lancers. When Latham was knocked down he managed to keep hold, take the flag to the ground with him and lay on top of it. As he lay there, trampled by jostling horses and jabbed by the lancers, he still managed to find the strength with his remaining arm to tear the sacred silk from the staff and stuff it in the front of his jacket before he lost consciousness.

The French and Poles were eventually driven off by the arrival of the British 7th Fusiliers and 48th Foot but not before most of Latham's battalion had been cut down, scattered or driven off towards the French lines as prisoners. A fusilier turned Latham over and retrieved the precious cloth but left Latham's battered body where it lay. The flag was returned to the headquarters of the Buffs after the battle was over with news of how it had been defended, apparently, to the death.

Latham, meanwhile, had regained consciousness amid the heaped corpses and crawled for two hours on his remaining hand and knees until he reached a river and stopped to slake his thirst. Here he was found by some British orderlies and taken to a convent serving as a field hospital, where the mangled remnant of his left arm was amputated and his other wounds patched up.

Not only did Latham recover from his wounds but he was eventually able to return to service with his regiment. With his uniform, by special dispensation, he wore a gold medallion engraved with the words 'I shall surrender it only with my life', paid for by contributions from his brother officers. He was later presented to the Prince Regent (later George IV) who personally paid for an eminent surgeon, Mr Carpuet, to use his new (one might say 'cutting-edge') techniques to reconstruct Latham's mutilated face.

Ensign Christie at Quatre Bras

At the Battle of Quatre Bras in June 1815, The British 44th (East Essex) Regiment were hard pressed by French cavalry. Ensign Christie, bearing one of the regiment's two prized colours (or flags), was attacked by a lancer. The Frenchman thrust his lance down into Christie's left eye, the point going on to pierce his tongue and penetrate his lower jaw before it was wrenched free again. The stubborn Ensign, however, did not let go of the flag staff and, as the Frenchman made another thrust, Christie threw himself on the ground on top of the colours, though a portion of the precious cloth was torn away on the tip of the lance. Some of Christie's fellow Essex boys arrived in the nick of time to save him before he could be skewered again where he lay, shooting the Frenchman and lifting him from his saddle on the points of their bayonets for good measure. Christie survived the wound and remained in the army.

This chasseur is no chicken

Of course the British had no monopoly on courage in the Napoleonic period. Even the Frenchmen of those days showed remarkable resilience. At the Battle of Eylua in East Prussia, which was fought on February 1807 amid deep snow and sudden blizzards, French cavalry were called upon to attack masses of Russian infantry and cavalry. In the desperate fighting, Lieutenant Rabusson of the Chasseurs à Cheval of the Imperial Guard was unhorsed and repeatedly bayoneted, seven times in his head and face, twice in the thigh, twice in the arms and three times in the chest for a total of fourteen wounds. A Russian hussar then rode up and attempted to spare his life by calling upon him to surrender but a still-defiant Rabusson refused. A blow from the hussar's sabre finally felled him and he was left for dead, lying unconscious in the snow. Despite the risk of hypothermia, the sub-zero temperatures probably saved his life by slowing the bleeding until he was found by French infantry hours later and carried to safety.[38]

Ernst Udet – within an ace of death

The men who took to the air during the First World War must all have been a little mad. Powered flight was only a few years old and the planes were little more than bundles of sticks and canvas tied up with piano wire and with an engine stuck on the front (or sometimes the back). Just to take off in one of these machines in peacetime was courting disaster, but to go to war in one was like kicking the Reaper in the backside and running off shouting 'catch me if you can boney'. Few teased Death quite so relentlessy as Ernst Udet. Nicknamed 'Kneckes' ('Titch'), he was initially rejected by the Imperial German Air Service on account of being barely 5 feet 2 inches tall, but once he was up and flying his career was an impressive series of successes punctuated with regular mishaps. He ended the war as

Germany's top-scoring *surviving* ace but it could so easily have been different.

His run of close calls began with just his second mission on 14 September 1915. Piloting a two-seater Aviatik, there was a loud twang and his plane banked steeply to one side as the main bracing wire between the upper and lower right wing came adrift. To get the aircraft flying level again Udet had to keep the rudder hard over all the time and his plucky observer, seated in front, had to climb out of his cockpit and sit far out on the lower wing with his legs dangling in the wind. Not daring to risk a change of direction (apart from the risk to his comrade, the right wings started flapping each time he tried to bank) they flew on over enemy territory towards neutral Switzerland. Before they reached the border, the extreme effort of wrestling with the controls took its toll on Udet and his strength was failing. The observer duly pulled himself back along the wing, clambered into his cockpit then smashed through the wooden partition so he could reach through with a now-bloody hand to help with the joystick. In this manner they eventually crossed the Swiss border, gliding in to land in a potato field as they had by then also run out of fuel. The local blacksmith repaired the broken part and they were able to fly home.

Ten days later, Titch took off on what was supposed to be an observation mission (spotting for the artillery), but the same observer had decided to take along some bombs just for fun. The feeble aircraft, already burdened by the addition of a primitive wireless set, was overloaded, went into a spin shortly after take off and crashed back onto the airfield. Luckily none of the bombs went off and the observer escaped with only minor bruises (he had climbed out of his cockpit again and was thrown clear on impact) although Udet was hospitalized for ten days. On his return to duty he was transferred to another squadron and there given seven days field punishment for endangering his observer! (His observer was an officer, while Udet was a private – in those early days the pilots were seen as mere chauffeurs to the officer observers).

As he returned to his new airfield from jail he was met by an observer officer who ordered him into the pilot's seat of a dilapidated aircraft being loaded up for a bombing mission. Avoiding enemy fighters near the intended target, they picked another likely looking spot, the officer opened the little hatch in the floor of his cockpit and started dropping bombs one at a time by hand. Soon, however, one struck the plane's fixed undercarriage and stuck there. It couldn't be left there, for if it did not explode in flight then it probably would on landing, so the officer did the obvious thing and stuck his leg through the hatch to kick it free. His thigh got stuck in the opening where it stayed while Udet performed a series of increasingly violent manouvres in the old plane to eventually dislodge the bomb and he was not released until they landed.

This time Udet was praised for his efforts but dispatched to a squadron of the new fighters (or scouts in period terminology), single-seaters purpose built and armed to destroy other aircraft. His solo career did not start well either, his very first air combat ending with his goggles shot off his face and his plane riddled with bullet holes. Titch was shot down or crashed at least another four times during the war, including once while trying to land next to an enemy plane he'd shot down in German territory before it could be destroyed by its pilot. The French airman had to pull Udet from the wreckage before the latter could take him prisoner over a shared cigarette. In addition there were various forced but safely-made landings due to engine trouble or landing to ask directions when lost. Another time he forced an RE-8 down and was just coming into land beside it when he realized the soldiers running and shooting towards him were all British and that he was behind enemy, not German lines as he had thought.

Blossoming as a fighter pilot, he was transferred to the famous 'Flying Circus' of the legendary Red Baron (Manfred von Richthofen). He survived brushes with legendary French aces Georges Guynemer, who gallantly let Udet go with a salute when he saw him hammering on his jammed guns, and Charles Nungesser (another flukey survivor whom we shall return to) who put some bullet holes through his flying suit. Even one of the sixty-three victories he racked up was actually a mishap as he destroyed the upper wing of a Sopwith Camel by unwittingly clipping it with his undercarriage as he came out of a loop.

The last, and perhaps jammiest, of Titch's wartime prangs came on 29 June 1918 when his damaged Fokker D.VII went into an uncontrollable spin. Finding he could not correct it he decided it was time to try out the parachute he had recently been issued (a new innovation). As he tried to make a controlled exit from the cockpit, the slipstream swept him back along the fuselage and past the tail, where his parachute harness snagged on the rudder. As the aircraft continued to plummet and spin earthwards, a frantic Udet eventually managed to tear away part of the rudder and fell free. The parachute worked and, despite being machine-gunned as he descended, he came down to earth intact. He was not safe quite yet though, since he landed amid an artillery barrage. As he rapidly exited the area he was twice blown over by the blast of near misses, the second of which lodged a stone in one of his buttocks. Just for good measure there were poisonous gas shells included in the bombardment through which he had to run for some 3 miles with no gas mask.

Yet again Udet had escaped to fly another day. Although he scored his last two kills on 19 September 1918, taking a bullet graze to the arm in the process, he was still flying combat missions at the Armistice on 11 November.

Defeated Germany was banned from having an air force by the Treaty of Versailles but Udet kept his hand in between the wars by crashing at least another nine times. Making an aviation film in Africa he had several notable escapades, including a forced landing on the savannah that left him for three days without food or water before being rescued, ironically, by the RAF. On one occasion, while engaged in the extremely low flying that was his speciality, a pouncing lion narrowly missed his aircraft but with its second leap tore a strip from the wing of the plane following. Another time, Ernst decided to take some ground footage and pointed out a rock as a reference point for a likely spot to land. Touching down, the rock turned out to be a rhino which took exception to the intrusion and attacked.

Fortunately for Britain, he rejoined the German air force in the 1930s, where he was largely responsible for the Luftwaffe's technical development and aircraft production. Promoted way beyond his administrative abilities he made decisions which definitely helped the Nazis lose the war. Still in love with flying and despite his senior status and progressive alcoholism (his personal aircraft were all modified with a mini-bar in the cockpit), he took every opportunity to be involved in the testing of new combat aircraft. Trying out the prototype of a new Heinkel dive bomber, he forgot the designer's warning that dive brakes had not yet been fitted. He nose-dived it at full speed, which caused the propeller and tail to come off. He bailed out too late for his parachute to work fully as his shoe got stuck in the pedals, hit the ground hard and was knocked unconscious. As concerned observers reached him he came round just long enough to pronounce the new aircraft a 'shit crate', ending its development instantly. In 1937 he also managed to crash and write off the prototype of a helicopter. Sadly (for the Allied cause) he finally decided to give the Grim Reaper a hand and committed suicide in 1941.

Charles Nungesser

Charles Nungesser, who, as mentioned above, crossed flightpaths with little Ernst Udet, was possibly the most wounded man in the First World War. Wounded some seventeen times, he crashed more often than the European economic system and the uncharitable might suggest he survived the war mainly because he spent so much time in hospital. On one occasion he took a shortcut by actually crashing directly into a field hospital (pleasing one of the patients already in there with a minor wound by breaking his legs, a 'Blighty one' severe enough to get him invalided safely home). To be fair, though, Nungesser never used his wounds as an excuse to shirk combat, on occasion having himself carried to his cockpit because he was unable to walk.

After the war, Nungesser tried to set up a private flying school but failed to attract enough students. I can't think why.

Poon Lim

At 1410hrs on 23 November 1942 the German submarine U-172 attacked a British merchant ship, *Ben Lomond*, as it sailed westward from Cape Town in South Africa to collect cargo in Dutch Guiana. *Ben Lomond* was struck by two torpedoes and sank rapidly some 750 miles off the coast of Brazil. Many of the fifty-five crew were killed by the explosions or went down with the ship. Poon Lim, a twenty-four-year-old Chinese steward, almost joined them when, leaving it late to jump overboard, he was sucked down by the vortex created as the 9,750-ton ship headed for the bottom but was saved by his life jacket. Surfacing in a slick of oil and debris, he saw other survivors in a life boat but was unable to reach them or make himself heard and they soon passed out of his sight. After bobbing around hopelessly for a couple of hours he found a life raft and managed to pull himself aboard.

The raft was about 8 feet square and had been thoughtfully stocked with a 40-litre container of fresh water, chocolate, tins of biscuits and a bag of sugar lumps. There were also some flares and smoke signals, hemp rope and an electric torch. When the water inevitably ran out Poon Lim resorted to catching rain water in the canvas covering of his life jacket. Biscuits and chocolate used up? No problem. Poon prised a nail from the raft and fashioned it into a fish hook which he used in conjunction with the hemp rope to catch fish. These were then filleted with a knife somehow fashioned from a biscuit tin and hung to dry on more hemp rope rigged up overhead. He also used the rope as a safety line around his wrist when he swam twice a day to keep in shape.

At a desperate low ebb after a storm had swept away his stock of dried fish and ruined his water with brine, he managed to catch a seagull, eat it raw and drink its blood, though not before it had inflicted some nasty cuts with its beak. The next seagull, he decided, was better used as bait for one of the sharks he had spotted. The bait worked and the shark was hauled aboard the raft but then fought ferociously for its life until Poon beat it to death with the water jug. As first priority he slaked his thirst by drinking blood from the shark's liver but took the time to dry its fins in the sun for later, a delicacy back home.

For the most part completely alone in the vastness of the ocean, Poon did spot other vessels: another German submarine and a cargo vessel which he later claimed had passed close but left him because he was Chinese. His hopes were raised again when US Navy patrol planes spotted him and dropped a buoy to mark his position, only to have another storm sweep him away from the area before he could be rescued. Eventually he noticed that the water was now a murky brown, suggesting he was nearing a coast. A few days later, on 5 April 1943 he was picked up 10 miles off the Brazilian coast by a fishing boat and was soon walking ashore, which he managed unaided. He had lost 9kg in weight and had an upset stomach but was otherwise in surprisingly good health and was discharged after four weeks in hospital. Returning to Britain via the USA he was awarded a British Empire Medal and his exploits soon formed part of a Royal Navy booklet on survival at sea, copies of which were stored on all British life rafts. After the war he re-crossed the Atlantic in happier circumstances, emigrating to the USA, where he died in 1991. His record of 133 days at sea on a raft still stands.

Freedom costs an arm and a leg

All of the above are made to look like real wimps beside the Rajput general, Rana Sanga, who ruled Mewar from 1509 to 1526. He united Rajasthan in resistance to the expansionist Mughals under Babur, in the process being wounded eighty times, including the loss of an arm and a leg.

Chapter 10

Siege the Day

The nature of sieges, in contrast to battles in the open, meant that attacker and defender alike could often take their time to improvise particularly innovative and devious means of getting one over on the enemy.

Philip V is caught short

One of the simplest solutions to the problem of getting into the enemy's fortified places was to put ladders against the wall and climb over. Obviously, if the enemy was alert and expecting you then it became a lot harder. If they didn't simply push your ladder over they could drop all sorts of nasties on you (as we shall see later), or even just wait till you were clambering over the parapet to knock you on the head.

Being a dynamic and generally capable commander, Philip V of Macedon (reigned 229–179 BC) understood all this, he had after all been king since the age of eight. That's why, when he wanted to capture the town of Melitea, he drove his army hard on a punishing forced march of several days and nights, arriving before the walls early one morning before the defenders even knew he was on his way. On Philip's order the Macedonian troops raced to the foot of the walls and propped up the ladders they had just lugged for so many miles, eager to swarm over the walls and fall upon the unsuspecting Meliteans. Unfortunately the ladders were all several feet too short and the army, which in its haste had marched without the encumbrance of more sophisticated siege equipment or the supplies for a sustained operation, had no choice but to slink away again.[39]

Philip's unpreparedness was due to his need for speed. Given more time, the Romans at the lengthy siege of Syracuse (in 214–212 BC, of which more soon) showed how it should be done. An envoy sent into the city under the pretence of negotiation took the opportunity to make a good estimate of the height of a single course of stones. It was then a simple matter to count the number of courses in the wall and calculate the total height needed for the ladders used in the final assault.

Hats off to the Persians

We have already met Croesus of Lydia who provoked a war with Cyrus the Great's Persia thanks to a mischievous answer from the oracle at Delphi. In the final stages of that war, the Persians had Croesus and his remaining forces bottled up in the acropolis of his capital, Sardis (in modern Turkey).* This stronghold was reported to be unassailable due to its strong walls and the natural strength of its position atop a steep-sided spur of Mount Tmolus.

The Persians sat scratching their heads beneath the towering edifice for two weeks. Cyrus promised to make a rich man of the first man over the walls but even with this incentive the ensuing massed assault on the least precipitous section of the walls was easily repulsed with heavy losses. The Persians might have been stymied for another two weeks or more if it had not been for an insignificant little mishap that befell one of the Lydian defenders. This chap was one of the few sentries deemed necessary on that part of the defences considered most impenetrable of all, built as it was along the top of the sheerest cliffs. When his helmet fell from his head and clattered its way down the rocks it was the kind of thing that could happen to anyone. Not everyone, though, would have been stupid enough to do what he did next. Probably thinking more of the punishment for losing a piece of kit than anything else, he promptly used his local knowledge to scamper down the apparently sheer cliff and back up again with his retrieved helmet, no doubt thinking how cleverly he had got away with it. His officers may not have seen but a Persian soldier by the name of Hyroeades had been watching it all with interest and made a mental note of the route taken. Eager to win the

---

* Many cities had an 'acropolis' (literally 'highest city') – a stronghold built on the highest ground within or adjoining the city's walls that could be used as a last line of defence and refuge even once the city itself had been captured. The remains of Sardis' acropolis are still impressive.

prize, he was soon leading an assault force up the way he had been unwittingly shown. The few guards on this sector were surprised and easily overwhelmed. Its defences breached, the rest of the acropolis soon fell and Croesus was captured.[40]

Scale the walls – Yashvanti, the living grappling hook

In the 1670s, the Muslim Mughals under Aurangzeb (1658–1707) already dominated most of India and were still attempting to expand their empire to the south. They were resisted by the Marathas, a Hindu movement which coalesced under the leadership of Shivaji (1627–80). Shivaji and his generals, though generally the underdogs in terms of numbers and equipment, proved to be very resourceful tacticians relying on guerrilla warfare launched from a network of secure fortresses. This resourcefulness can be illustrated no more clearly than by the recapture of the formidable defences of Kondana Fort in 1670.

The fort's main defence was its location atop a precipice, which rendered impractical the conventional siege techniques of escalade (assault by troops climbing up ladders) or battering a breach with artillery, an arm in which the Marathas were at this time still weak anyway. Undeterred, a Maratha force under Tanaji Malusare was able to scale the sheer cliffs and gain a foothold on the walls by tying a rope to a large lizard named Yashvanti, who was then induced to climb the walls, or was perhaps thrown over them. He was almost certainly a Bengal monitor lizard (*Varanus bengalensis*) known locally as *ghorpad*, which can grow up to 175cm long and can weigh up to 7.2kg. Being named, he was presumably a tame pet, perhaps even specially trained for this role. Whether through training or just seeking refuge, Yashvanti crawled into a crack in the rock and braced himself, effectively acting like a living grappling hook, his grip proving strong enough for the human attackers to scale the walls.

The ensuing battle was fierce, both Tanaji Malusare and his son being killed, but the fort was taken. Shivaji, distraught at the loss of his brave general reportedly said 'We have gained the fort, but lost the lion' and the fort has ever since been known as Sinhagad (the Lion's Fort). It is not recorded whether Yashvanti survived.

Twisted fire starters

If you can't get your men over the walls why not send in birds to start fires? This is one of the suggestions to be found in the *Arthashastra*, an ancient Indian manual on the art of war. The idea is for the besieger to trap some of the birds that have their nests within the city (crows, vultures and pigeons are among the possibilities listed), tie some form of incendiary to their tails and release them so that they fly back to their nests, carrying fire to timber-framed and thatched buildings within.

The incendiary itself might consist of 'flammable powders' (*agniyoga*), obviously some spontaneously combustible compound (naptha or phosphorous based?) which speaks of advanced scientific understanding; or 'a splinter of fire kept in the body of a dried fish', which doesn't. If birds aren't available, monkeys can be used. If you have a spy within the city you have even more choice since he can attach the fire to the tails of mongooses, cats or dogs and set them running across the thatched rooves. Fires breaking out at multiple points within the city could destroy valuable buildings, such as grain stores and arsenals, or cause sufficient distraction and panic among the defenders to allow a well-timed assault to succeed easily. Of course they could also burn down the city you were hoping to capture for yourself.

The *Arthashstra* is attributed to Kautilya, trusted minister of the mighty Chandragupta Maurya, the empire builder who chased Alexander the Great's successors out of northern India and Pakistan in the second century BC. It is a veritable mine of tactical tips but it does not cite actual examples of these methods being used and we cannot know which were actually tried and with what success. The fire bird trick cited here is one of the more bizarre and might easily be dismissed as a product of Kautilya's imagination if it were not for independent corroboration from an incident far removed in time and place.

It is highly unlikely, if not strictly impossible, that the Norwegian Harald Hardrada had read the *Arthashastra* so he must have come up with the idea himself. He is now generally remembered only for his part in 1066 and all that and his death in that year at the Battle of Stamford Bridge but, before becoming king of Norway, Harald had been one of the boldest viking adventurers ever to ply the seas, which is how he came to be laying siege to a town in Sicily. Apparently a giant of a man (anything over 6 feet in those under-nourished days) and a ferocious fighter, he was evidently blessed with brains as well as brawn. The town was heavily fortified; Harald had no means of breaching its strong walls and didn't want to wait for starvation to do its work. He noticed that sparrows flew out of the town every day to feed in the fields, returning at dusk to their nests in the thatched houses. Harald set his men to capturing a large number of the sparrows, presumably with nets, then tying lighted sticks to their tails before releasing them. Exactly as planned, the poor birds flew back to their nests, the town was soon reduced to ashes and the surviving inhabitants surrendered to Harald.[41]

'Baby on the way!'

During the Jewish revolt of AD 66–70, the Romans used their cata-pults (nicknamed 'onagers' after a kind of wild ass because they had such a kick) to launch lumps of stone weighing over 50lbs (about 25kg) at or over the walls of rebellious cities. In a scene reminiscent of the siege of Minas Tirith in the film version of *Lord of the Rings*, Josephus, commanding the garrison of Jotopata, tells us they could hurl these 400 yards or more with a terrifying rushing sound and devastating effect. He not only says these projectiles 'carried away battlements and knocked corners off towers', but gives two grisly illustrations of the point:

> One of the men standing near Josephus on the rampart got into the line of fire and had his head knocked off by a stone, his skull being flung like a pebble from a sling more than 600 yards; and when a pregnant woman was struck in the belly on leaving her house at daybreak, the unborn child was carried away 100 yards. [Josephus, *The Jewish War*, III]

It may have been rumour of the latter incident that inspired the grim humour of the defenders at the slightly later siege of Jerusalem. Josephus, still an eyewitness but by this time from the Roman side, explains that they were using white stone which flashed in the sunlight. Every time one was launched, lookouts posted on the city's towers would shout the warning 'baby on the way!' in time for everyone nearby to scatter for cover. The Romans soon cottoned on and started darkening the stones before firing making them hard to spot. Killjoys.

Corbulo's calling card

A single shot from a catapult proved decisive when the Romans, under Gnaeus Domitius Corbulo, arrived outside Tigranocerta, the capital of Armenia, in AD 55. This was to be the culmination of a triumphant campaign for the Roman general who had already marched across most of Armenia, taking the country's second city, storming various fortresses and generally crushing all resistance. According to one account, the Tigranocertans, already abandoned by their king, had previously sent a delegation to meet the approaching Corbulo, telling him the city's gates were open and the city would welcome him without a fight.[42]

When the Romans stomped up, however, the gates were closed and it looked like the Armenians might make a fight of it after all. As the legions went to work setting up their siege engines, Corbulo decided to announce his arrival. He ordered a chap called Vadandus, an Armenian nobleman captured earlier in the campaign, to be decapitated and his severed head fired from a ballista, a kind of siege catapult. Vadandus' head cleared the battlements and, as luck would have it, landed slap bang in the middle of the Armenian leaders as they were debating whether to resist or not. Their meeting was swiftly concluded and 'they made haste to surrender'.[43]

Mine, all mine

If the enemy's walls were too well defended to go over them, one could always try going under them. Mining, that is digging tunnels under the enemy's walls, was a common siege technique. Usually the idea was not actually to dig your way directly in and send troops through the tunnel; rather the idea was to dig a mine toward a section of the defences, propping it up with timber to stop it collapsing. Once directly beneath the targeted section of wall or tower, combustible material was packed in (at the siege of Rochester in 1215, King John used the fat of forty pigs – lots of crackling) and the miners set it aflame before legging it. When the props burnt through, the tunnel collapsed, bringing down the tower or section of wall above – this is the literal meaning of being 'undermined'.

It was a very effective technique but not without its hazards. Defenders developed ingenious techniques for detecting mining activity and locating the tunnels. Metal rods were driven into the ground within the walls, which would resonate with the vibration of the digging, or pans of water were placed and watched for the tell-tale ripples like that scene in *Jurassic Park*. Once they knew roughly where the besiegers were digging, the defenders would drive their own tunnel, or countermine, into the earth. If they could break into the enemy tunnel they could attack the miners. Such subterranean scuffles, however, were risky and claustrophobic affairs and other ways of driving out the enemy were sought.

At Dura Europos, a fortress on the Euphrates, the war-ravaged border between the Roman and Persian empires, archaeologists have excavated mines used in the siege of AD 256. In the tunnels they found the skeletons of one Persian and nineteen Roman soldiers. Chemical residues suggest they were asphyxiated by the smoke from burning bitumen and sulphur, which would have turned to sulphuric acid in their lungs. This was one of the more practical and sophisticated methods, as the following example will show by way of contrast.

Early in 72 BC, a Roman army laid siege to the town of Themyscira in Pontus. (The historian Appian tells us the city was named after one of the Amazons, the legendary female warriors, while superhero comic geeks will recognize that the name was appropriately used as the home of Wonder Woman – don't think she was involved here though!) The besiegers set to undermining the wall with gusto and the defenders to countermining with equal vigour, digging 'tunnels so large that great subterranean battles could be fought in them'. Imagine the surprise and horror on the faces of the Roman miners when wild (or at least slightly miffed) bears started dropping through holes in the roof of their tunnel. The defenders had dug their countermines immediately above, broken openings down into the attacking mine and prodded and bundled the beasts down upon the startled diggers. Beehives soon followed, filling the tunnel with swarms of angry insects to sting man and beast alike. The Romans could not bear it and buzzed off, abandoning the siege.

Getting the enemy on the run

Around 595 BC, Clisthenes of Sicyon laid siege to the town of the Crisaeans which received its water through pipes or conduits. Clisthenes cut off the water supply and presumably could have simply waited until dehydration took its toll. Instead, perhaps through impatience or simply a sense of mischief, he added a subtle twist. Once the Crisaeans were really thirsty, he restored the flow. The parched inhabitants happily guzzled the precious liquid, unaware that Clisthenes had spiked it with hellebore, a powerful laxative. With all the defenders incapacitated by diarrhoea, the Sicyonian troops were easily able to storm and capture the town.[44]

A river ran through it – Mantinea, 385 BC

At the siege of Mantinea in 385 BC, the besieging Spartan king, Agesipolis, did not attempt to cut off the water supply of the besieged inhabitants, but increased it. Having encircled the city with the intention of starving it into surrender, he learned that its store houses were particularly well stocked from a good harvest, so the inhabitants were likely to be able to hold out a long time. As a large river ran through the city, they also had plenty of water to drink and they were about to get more than they could handle.

Agesipolis dammed up the river downstream of the city causing the river to flood. According to Xenophon's account, the water steadily rose above the foundations of the houses and of the city wall. The walls were made of dried mud brick:

> As the moisture began to affect the lower layers of bricks, the upper ones also were weakened; first cracks began to appear in the walls and then signs of collapse. The Mantineans tried for some time to prop it up with timbers and did everything they could think of to prevent the tower from collapsing. But they could not keep pace with the effects of the water.
>
> [Xenophon, *Hellenika*, V.2.4]

The Mantineans, seeing the watery writing on the wall, surrendered shortly thereafter, being forced to pull down what was left of their soggy defences as part of the peace terms.

Casilinum, 216 BC

A river also played its part in a nice little battle of wits during the siege of Casilinum in 216 BC. The famous Hannibal was besieging the Roman-allied town on the banks of the Volturnus in Italy. The siege had been going on for some time and several direct assaults gallantly beaten off by the small garrison but supplies were running out. Gracchus, commanding a Roman field force further upstream, had too few troops to risk attacking the mighty Hannibal but when reports reached him that some of the besieged were throwing themselves from the battlements to avoid a slow death by starvation he came up with a plan to help them.

Having first got a message explaining his plan through to the defenders*, Gracchus had his men fill large jars with wheat and, under cover of darkness, push them off into river. The current carried them along, through the Carthaginian siege lines and down to the city where the defenders were waiting to intercept them. This worked perfectly for three nights in a row but on the fourth night some of the jars washed up on the riverbank near the Carthaginians' positions, alerting them to what was going on. The next night Hannibal posted sentries along the river and these intercepted the jars. According to Frontinus book of stratagems, he may have suspended a chain across the river just below the surface to catch the bobbing jars, though Livy's fuller account does not mention this.[45]

His ruse thwarted, Gracchus was not yet ready to give up. He now had nuts gathered and thrown loose onto the water. The nuts again floated down, riding too high in the water to snare on the chain, too small to be easily spotted in the dark and too numerous and scattered to be intercepted by sentries in any case. The people of Casilinum, again forewarned, were able to gather them by 'hurdles (i.e. wicker fence panels, commonly used for animal pens) placed across the stream'.

While ingeniously delivered, the nuts were not however sufficient to sustain the defiance of the besieged for long. The historian Livy

---

*Probably because the river flowed right by the town and, according to Livy's acount, had recently flooded (presumably making the banks boggy), Hannibal's blockade was evidently not complete enough to stop messengers slipping in and out.

says the garrison were reduced to eating 'mice and other creatures', then to chewing leather thongs and the hide coverings of their shields softened in boiling water. Having consumed everything they could within the walls, they started venturing just beyond them and 'dug up every kind of root and green-stuff they could find in the bank beneath the walls'. In response, Hannibal then had the ground right up to the walls ploughed over until not so much as a blade of grass was left to forage (an operation presumably undertaken under covering fire from his archers and slingers). The garrison responded with a bit of bluff that signalled their intention to sit tight for a while yet – they sprinkled turnip seeds into the furrows so helpfully ploughed for them. Exasperated by their defiance, Hannibal is supposed to have cried 'What? Am I to sit here until *that* comes up?' Despairing of securing the unconditional surrender of the town any time soon he offered them a deal and the garrison, the half that were still breathing, were allowed to leave hungry but unharmed on the payment of a ransom.

Archimedes and the defence of Syracuse

When a Roman army besieged the great Sicilian city of Syracuse in early 213 BC, its commander, the consul Marcus Claudius Marcellus, was probably quite confident of victory, despite the towering walls. Whilst in open battles the Roman armies of this period were not the invincible killing machines often imagined, they had a fantastic record in sieges. Generally speaking, once a Roman army settled down outside a city, it didn't leave until the place was captured and thoroughly looted, usually with a large proportion of the population ending up dead or marched off in chains to a slave market. Moreover, the city, which until recently had been a Roman ally, had recently been wracked by political chaos, factional splits, coups and counter-coups, so it probably seemed ripe for the taking.

However, if Marcellus entertained any ideas of victory coming quickly, he had not reckoned on the genius of one man within: the famous mathematician Archimedes. He might now be most famous for having a light-bulb moment in the bath and running naked through the streets shouting '*eureka*!' (roughly 'I've got it!'), but this old flasher was an eminent boffin of the first order. When he wasn't formulating the scientific principles that still underpin modern engineering he was putting his talents to practical use, devising war machines for the defence of the city.

Syracuse was a coastal city, the Mediterranean waters actually lapping against one section of its walls. Marcellus sent a large portion of his force to attack the city from the landward side while he led a seaborne assault with his fleet. Both prongs soon discovered that Archimedes had overseen the construction of a well-thought out array of catapults which began bombarding them with rocks and causing heavy casualties. As such machines, which lobbed their stones in a high arcing trajectory, could not be quickly adjusted to different ranges, the usual defence in such a situation would be to close with the enemy quickly and out of their 'killing field' or 'beaten zone'. Archimedes however, had arranged different batteries calibrated for different ranges which successively took up the bombardment as the Romans drew nearer, maintaining a constant rain of deadly missiles. Some of the stones may have been 100 pounds in weight. Those ships that got too close for the stone lobbers, were greeted by powerful engines firing huge darts on a flat trajectory through loopholes cut through the base of the walls, easily capable of pinning a soldier's shield to his body.

Archimedes did not invent stone-throwers or bolt-shooters; these were conventional siege weapons employed in a particularly well thought out way. They were enough to stop the landward attack in its tracks, but the seaborne attack did approach right inshore, close to the base of the walls, where Marcellus brought some impressive kit of his own into play. He had a fleet of sixty-eight quinqueremes, the standard heavy warship of the day. Most of these carried an assault force of soldiers plus archers to provide covering fire, but eight ships had been converted into four giant catamarans by lashing them together in pairs (or in one account, all eight were joined into one huge catamaran). Each catamaran provided the base for a huge contraption known as a sambuca, because it resembled a musical instrument of the same name. It was essentially a 4ft-wide ladder, long enough to reach the top of the city walls, and protected by wicker screens. When the ships were close enough, the ladders were to be raised against the walls by means of ropes and pulleys rigged from the ships masts. A small guard of soldiers would be raised with the ladder, protected by the screens along its sides, to beat back the defenders on the walls and ensure it was properly lodged against the battlements before more troops clambered up.

We don't know exactly how many of Marcellus' ships made it through the barrage to close with the city walls but Archimedes had prepared some nasty surprises for them. Long beams, hitherto invisible to the attackers, now swung out from the battlements, pivoting on universal joints. Rigged like cranes with ropes, pulleys and counterweights (levers were Archimedes' big thing), they carried heavy lead weights which they dropped onto the Roman vessels, shattering their timbers. It was these, it seems, that did for the sambuca ships but other ships fell victim to an interesting variation on the theme. Instead of just dropping weights, some of the cranes let down what the ancient historians described as an iron hand (*ferrea manus*) to catch hold of the front end of the enemy ship. Fun as is to imagine an actual mechanical gripping hand, it was more probably a heavy, iron grappling hook or giant barbed harpoon which, when dropped, would smash through the upper deck. When the device was raised again it lifted the ship's prow clear of the water until the vessel stood on its stern. Given that a fully manned quinquereme weighed approximately 100 metric tons, Archimedes' engineering skills are fully revealed.

One of the more colourful ancient accounts, that of Plutarch, describes the stricken ships being 'spun round by means of windlasses situated inside the city and dashed against the steep cliffs and rocks which jutted under the walls, with great loss of life to the crews'. This was probably unnecessary, as just dropping the ships again was sufficient, as the more sober account of our earliest source, Polybius, clearly describes:

> The result was that some of the vessels heeled over and fell on their sides, and others capsized, while the majority when their bows were let fall from a height plunged under water and filled, and thus threw all into confusion.   [Polybius, VIII.6]

Impressive as these well-attested inventions were, there are those that attribute a truly incredible weapon to Archimedes. Now sometimes touted as 'Archimedes' death ray' it was said to be an array of mirrors, possibly highly-polished shields, used to focus the sun's rays on Marcellus' ships to set them ablaze. Unfortunately, the evidence for this is very tenuous. The historians of the war do not mention it, the earliest reference being in a scientific treatise on optics by Galen, written around four hundred years after the event. Modern experiments to test the viability of such a 'death ray' have been inconclusive but on balance it seems that flaming missiles flung from catapults would have been an incomparably more practical option.

Even without the death ray, Marcellus was dismayed at his vessels being handled in this way while the defenders apparently laughed at him from the walls as they did it. Marcellus tried to put a brave face on it, wittily remarking that Archimedes had used his ships to ladle seawater into his cups but then whipped his sambuca band out of the party, but the Romans had to abandon the assault and settle down for a lengthy, methodical siege.

Syracuse held out for the best part of three years. Her awesome outer defences finally fell to the simplest of techniques. Waiting until the night of a Syracusan religious festival, when most of the city's defenders were drunk and/or asleep, Marcellus sent an assault party over the landward walls using simple ladders and these overwhelmed the few sentries and opened the gates. Though part of the city held out a while longer, it was only a matter of time before the whole place was in Roman hands. Archimedes was killed in the traditional looting and killing spree that followed. Apparently he was still busy working out some complex mathematical problem when one of the rampaging Romans found him and, ignoring the boffin's tetchy remarks not to interrupt his calculations, killed him on the spot.

The winds of change

In 1848 Europe was aflame with revolutionary, nationalist ideals, and nowhere more so than Italy, much of which was under the oppressive heel of the Austrian Habsburg Empire. On 22 March of that year, a plucky band of revolutionaries led by Daniel Manin led a non-violent coup in Venice, declaring independence from their foreign overlords. The coup was very popular, most of the surrounding districts joined the revolt and the ancient Venetian Republic was resurrected with Manin as its leader. The Austrians, of course, did not take this laying down and soon had the city surrounded and besieged by a fleet offshore and an army under their Field Marshal Radetzky (to whom Johann Strauss dedicated his famous Radetzky March). It was a one-sided contest. The Venetian forces were pitiful and Manin, no great strategist, squandered every opportunity to make common cause with Austria's other enemies. The end result was inevitable but the Austrians couldn't just waltz in (not least because Venice's location amid a maze of lagoons made it difficult for a heavily-equipped army to approach). It was not until late August 1849 that the combination of bombardment and starvation finally forced the Republic's surrender.

On 12 July 1849, frustrated that bombardment by conventional artillery was not having quick enough results, Radetzky tried a new weapon suggested by one of his artillery officers. He ordered the release of 200 unmanned hot-air balloons, each carrying a bomb which was to be released over the beleaguered city by a timed fuse. This was an ingenious plan and the novelty of an aerial attack might have had a significant impact on Venetian morale if things had gone to plan. An eyewitness account suggests the actual result was not quite what Radetzky had in mind.

> The balloons appeared to rise to about 4,500ft. Then they exploded in midair or fell into the water, or, blown by a sudden southeast wind, sped over the city and dropped on the besiegers. Venetians, abandoning their homes, crowded into the streets and squares to enjoy the strange spectacle. ... When a cloud of smoke appeared in the air to mark an explosion, all clapped and shouted. Applause was greatest when the balloons blew over the Austrian forces and exploded, and in such cases the Venetians added cries of 'Bravo!' and 'Good appetite!'[46]

Despite this, the experiment was repeated on 22 August with similar results. Though the Venetians did surrender two days later, this seems to be coincidental. It seems Radetzky's faith in this new technology was over-inflated.

Catch that pigeon – the Siege of Paris, 1870–71

The Franco-Prussian war began with the French declaring war on Prussia on 19 July 1870 but they had been deliberately goaded into this and it was the Prussians who immediately went on the offensive, leading an alliance of other German states. The French resisted the German invaders in the style to which we are now accustomed and, just over six weeks later, Emperor Napoleon III and his army surrendered at the Battle of Sedan (2 September 1870). In Paris, however, the French defiantly declared the Third Republic. The new government hastily tried to organize national resistance to continue the war even as the city was swiftly surrounded and besieged by the Germans.

This time it was the defenders who turned to hot air balloons. The German blockade made it increasingly difficult to keep in touch with the other as-yet-unoccupied areas of France, where, it was hoped, new armies were being mustered to march to the capital's rescue. A professional balloonist, Jules Derouft, offered his services and made the first flight on 23 September. As he cleared the German siege lines with his cargo of mail he cheekily dropped calling cards on the enemy.

Realizing they had found a good way of sneaking stuff out of Paris, more flights ensued. These were followed by the realization that the prevailing winds that carried the balloons away from Paris were not going to bring any of them back – it was a one-way-only service. This suited Leon Gambetta, the head of the new Third Republic, just fine and he heroically booked his place on a flight out on 7 October, leaving the remaining defenders to it while he escaped to carry on the resistance from Tours in southwest France. Most of the passengers on later flights were carrier pigeons which would then be able to fly home carrying return mail. Five dogs were also airlifted out in this way, the plan being that their intended recipients would send them to find their way home bearing top secret data on microfilm. None of these canine couriers made it back.

Comical as they may seem, these balloon missions were no laughing matter for their human crews. Shortage of suitable materials and expertise meant most of the craft were flimsy and poorly made. The one-way nature of the traffic meant the supply of experienced pilots was quickly exhausted and the fact that most flights were made at night (because the Prussians had quickly invented the first anti-aircraft gun) didn't help. Of the sixty-six flights made, only fifty-eight landed safely and one of those had been carried off course to Norway, some 800 miles distant!

Unfortunately, it was all in vain. The news brought back by the pigeons was all bad, generally consisting of more French cities lost and the defeat of the Republic's hastily-recruited new armies. Paris itself fell on 28 January 1871, surrendering to the Germans who had officially united ten days previously to form the Empire of Germany, with Prussia's King Wilhelm I as its first Kaiser.

Back to basics – the capture of Fort Douamont

In February 1916, Erich von Falkenhayn, the German Chief of Staff, launched a major offensive towards the French city of Verdun. Verdun was protected by a ring of state-of-the-art strongpoints of which Fort Douamont was one. This pinnacle of defensive architecture was very different from the battlemented walls and towering citadels that had posed such obstacles to the armies of ancient times. Most of the fortress complex was underground, buried beneath several feet of steel-reinforced concrete to protect it against the heaviest enemy artillery. All that showed above ground were armoured domes with openings for defensive machine guns and observation. The fort's main armament was a pair of huge revolving gun turrets, each sporting a heavy 155mm howitzer, which could actually be retracted when not firing so they lay flush with the surrounding surface of the fort. The whole thing was protected by a ditch edged with barbed wire and railings to delay infantry while they were swept by machine guns firing from embrasures (small openings for guns). The Verdun forts had been touted in pre-war years as impregnable. Even though by 1916 one of its big guns and some of its defensive armament had been removed for use elsewhere, Douamont was expected to be a tough nut to crack. Yet it was to fall with virtually no resistance on 25 February, just five days into Falkenhayn's offensive. What devilish new weapon had 'les Bosches' come up with?

Well, it consisted of a small section of German infantry led by a twenty-four-year-old sergeant fighting their way through the French infantry positions covering the approach to Douamont and making it to the fort's ditch. They had just cut through the barbed wire when Sergeant Kunze was actually blown into the ditch by an exploding shell but his men soon took cover there too. They were not raked by any of the machine guns poking from embrasures which seemed not to be manned. Kunze had his men form a pyramid and he simply climbed in through one of these little windows. Only two of his men would follow him but this proved plenty. Wandering along the empty maze of corridors they came to the main gun position. The French gunners were having such a good time lobbing high explosive at some target in the far distance that they were oblivious to the Germans right behind them. They were quickly taken prisoner. The intrepid trio of Germans then explored a bit more until they found most of the remaining garrison in a hall, listening to a lecture on tactics of all things. Sergeant Kunze simply closed the door and locked them in. The fort seemingly captured, the Germans then found the canteen and helped themselves to a hearty meal. The party was spoiled a little when the fort's big gun recommenced firing as a new crew turned up for their shift, but by then officers from Kunze's regiment had arrived with reinforcements and the fort was soon fully secured.

For the momentous capture of this strategically significant fort, two of these Johnny-come-lately officers received the Pour Le Merite, the German equivalent of a Victoria Cross, while poor Sergeant Kunze's initiative went unrewarded.[47]

Chapter 11

Stranger Things Happen at Sea

The sinking of the Mary Rose – who left the doors open?

When Henry VIII succeeded to the English throne in 1509 he inherited a modest navy of just five major warships. Being intent on the traditional royal pastime of making war on the French, he immediately set about building a bigger and more modern fleet. Foremost of these new ships was the *Mary Rose*, one of the first ships to be armed with a broadside of cannon (that is the guns were ranged along the side of the vessel, firing through gunports cut in her sides). Completed probably in 1511, Henry's new flagship made a good start to her career by sinking the French flagship near Brest in 1512. By the time she went in for a major refit in 1536 she was a veteran of several wars against the French and their Scottish allies, with a generally successful record.

When she rejoined the fleet at Portsmouth in 1545 she had been replaced as the admiral's flagship by the larger *Henry Grace a Dieu* but now carried the flag of the vice admiral, Sir George Carew. In July a huge French fleet of some 200 French ships entered the Solent (the straits separating the Isle of Wight from the English mainland), landing troops to invade the Isle of Wight, and threatening Portsmouth itself. The English fleet, numbering only about eighty ships, came out to face this grave threat on 18 July.

The first day's engagement was a tentative affair of long-range gunnery duels with little damage to either side. That night the admiral of the fleet, Viscount Lisle, invited his senior officers to dine aboard his flagship. Vice Admiral Carew attended and may have taken a liking to the admiral's fancy plates, since a couple of them somehow found their way back to the *Mary Rose* with him. It is pure speculation to suggest that the effects of the dinner party played any part in the tragic events of the following day.

Battle resumed the following day amid a flat calm. The French fleet contained some oared galleys and these were sent forward to harass the English ships, which, being dependent upon the wind, were becalmed and unable to manoeuvre effectively to bring their broadsides to bear. Towards evening, the *Mary Rose* suddenly heeled over and sank and French accounts naturally claimed the guns of her galleys had sunk her.

Yet English sources suggest the *Mary Rose* was not directly engaged, and certainly not significantly damaged, by the galleys. Mystery still surrounds the exact causes but it seems a blunder was made in handling the ship, causing her to heel dangerously far over to starboard as soon as she raised full sail to try to catch a breath of wind. According to an eyewitness, none other than the brother of Vice Admiral Carew, the blame lay with the indiscipline of the crew. He quotes his brother, among his last words, calling them 'the sort of knaves whom he could not rule'. It was not that they weren't experienced, indeed the prestigious ship seems to have attracted an overqualified crew. Carew's biographer claimed there were a hundred master mariners on board 'the worst of them being able to be a master in the best ship in the realm'. These experts all thought they knew best and proved impossible to command:

> these so maligned and disdained one another, that refusing to do that which they should do, were careless to do that which was most needful and necessary.[48]

Among those things that were most needful and necessary was the small matter of closing the lower gun ports. As the ship continued to heel over, these open hatches dipped below the surface and the sea flooded in, quickly causing the ship to capsize. All but a couple of dozen of the 500 or so men aboard went to the bottom of the Solent with the *Mary Rose*, where they lay undisturbed until the ship, and Admiral Lisle's stolen plates, were raised in 1982.

Vasa, Vasa, everywhere ...

Sweden also boasts a resurrected man of war which attracts thousands of visitors a year. The Swedes are obviously very proud of her but it is hard to see why, since the *Vasa*, unlike *Mary Rose*, did not exactly have an illustrious career. In fact it must be about the shortest and most humiliating career of any warship, she was only a few minutes into her maiden voyage (10 August 1628) when a modest gust of wind caused her to roll over and sink just 390 feet (120 meters) from the shore.

Vasa was built on the orders of King Gustavus Adolphus, the ferocious 'Lion of the North', to bolster his Baltic Sea fleet. She was to be bigger and more powerful than any previous Swedish ship, built not only to fight but to be impressive to Sweden's enemies and rivals. It was basically a big boy's toy.

Sailing ships, with their towering masts, have a tendency to top-heaviness but one of the ways ship designers could minimize this in a two-decker was to mount the largest, heaviest guns on the lower deck and lighter ones on the upper. *Vasa*'s designers seem to have known this, the gun ports on the lower deck being designed for 24-pdrs, while the upper gun ports appear to have been originally intended for 12-pdrs.* But most boys will agree that if a toy has guns on it, and all the best boys' toys do, then it might as well have the biggest guns possible. Someone apparently decided to mount 24-pdrs on both decks and this may have contributed significantly to the ship's instability. Apparently her unsteadiness had been noticed while she was still fitting out in harbour but nobody had the nerve to tell an impatient Gustavus that his new toy was flawed and the remedial measures were restricted to fervent prayer and finger-crossing.

When *Vasa*'s big day came, the whole of Stockholm was out to watch and, more importantly, many dignitaries from foreign governments, just the sort of people Gustavus wanted to impress. She was moored in the lee of the city, so she cast off in the gentlest of breezes and eased away, resplendent with flags on every masthead and gun ports open ready to fire a farewell salute. Unfortunately, as she left the shelter of the city she was exposed to a slightly stronger breeze which was enough to make her lean hard over to port. As with *Mary Rose*, the open gun ports made an easy entry for the sea

---

* The classification refers to the weight of the balls they fired, not the cannon itself; a 24-pdr actually weighed about a ton.

and she went over and down. On the plus side, the crew did not have far to swim to safety and the majority survived. Gustavus, who was not actually present, being busy fighting a war, was predictably furious when he heard and demanded that the guilty be punished. A royal inquest was held but surprisingly failed to pin the blame on anyone.

Dazzling incompetence

On 19 April 1907, the destroyer HMS *Ariel* was one of five destroyers tasked to make a mock attack on Valetta, Malta, to test the defences of the Grand Harbour, which was then a major British naval base. The attack was to be made at night and the cunning plan called for Lieutenant Lancelot Turton to take *Ariel* in close to the outer coastal defences to draw their attention while the other four ships slipped stealthily into the Grand Harbour.

At 10.00pm Turton duly did his duty, approaching close to the shore at high speed and succeeded in catching the watchful eye of the defenders – a little too well. Searchlights from the shore forts were immediately turned upon *Ariel*, dazzling Turton and the other officers on the bridge. Temporarily blinded, they did not see the breakwater toward which they were steaming until it was too late. The collision buckled *Ariel*'s bow, put her telegraphs out of action and jammed her steering. HMS *Bruizer* came to assist and tried to tow her clear but the cable broke and the current carried *Ariel* towards the rocky shore. Fortunately *Bruizer* did manage to take off all *Ariel*'s crew bar one man before she ran aground and was wrecked on the rocks.[49]

Mona loser

In the First World War, the British tried all sorts of tactics to counter the new-fangled threat of the German U-boats and their cowardly, underhand lurking beneath the waves. One wheeze they tried was to take a small, defenceless little boat, just the sort of thing the dastardly enemy would like to attack, and have it sit in U-boat infested waters as a decoy, while a valiant British submarine stealthily lay in wait beneath the waves nearby.

This was the plan when the Royal Navy purchased *Mona*, a small sailing vessel, at Malta. Put under the command of a Lieutenant Harold Watts of the Royal Naval Reserve, and for some reason given the codename *Zeus*, she teamed up with the submarine *E.2* and headed for the coast of Sicily. On 6 July 1917 she soon attracted a German U-boat which surfaced nearby.* Unfortunately, as the U-boat approached, *E.2*'s conning tower broke above the choppy water and was spotted by the German, who submerged and made a run for safety at full speed to escape the ambush.

Shortly after, *Mona* lost contact with *E.2* and, now feeling rather vulnerable, Lieutenant Watts decided to head south, back toward Malta. As *Mona* sailed along, a nervous lookout sighted a submarine surfacing a short distance astern. Convinced this was the U-boat sneaking up on them, Watts decided that his duty now lay in avoiding capture and decided to abandon ship, ordering that *Mona* be scuttled for good measure lest she fall into enemy hands. His orders were efficiently carried out and *Mona* went to the bottom, her crew being picked up shortly after by a passing Japanese destroyer (on our side in the First World War). They only learned later that this had been completely unnecessary as the submarine turned out to be their old friend *E.2* who had been tailing them as planned all along.[50]

What goes around comes around

USS *Tang* was the most successful American submarine of the Second World War (and thus the most successful ever, so far). This achievement is all the more remarkable given that her active career lasted only nine months and two days and she made only five patrols.

The *Balao*-class vessel began her first hunting trip on 22 January 1944, departing Pearl Harbor for the waters around the Mariana Islands, and made an auspicious start by bagging five Japanese ships. Her second patrol proved fruitless but a combination of the

---

*Submarines often attacked on the surface, especially if they wanted to use their deck-mounted gun rather than waste a torpedo on a small vessel. Indeed, German U-boat commanders had a good record of politely warning merchant vessels that they were about to be sunk and inviting them to take to their life boats.

skill of her crew and good fortune saw her third patrol reap a bumper harvest. This time she sent ten more ships to the bottom, including two sunk accidentally by torpedoes that had missed their intended victims. Her fourth patrol, stalking the waters off Japan itself, added five more to the tally of ships sunk by *Tang*'s torpedoes plus a yacht wrecked by fire from her 5-inch deck gun.

Tang's skipper, Lieutenant Commander Richard H. O'Kane, must have been full of confidence when she slipped out of Pearl Harbor for the fifth and final time on 24 Sept 1944, carrying her usual complement of twenty-four torpedoes. This time she headed for the waters around Formosa (now Taiwan) and it was business as usual when the steel assassin sent two more Japanese freighters to Davy Jones' locker. Then, on 23 October, O'Kane sighted a convoy of four cargo ships and a troop transport protected by escorts. Waiting for the cover of darkness, O'Kane audaciously made a surface run past the escort screen (submarines were faster when surfaced), to get a crack at the crucial cargo ships. Firing off multiple torpedoes in quick succession, three of the freighters were quickly sunk or set ablaze. Illuminated by the flames, the submarine was spotted by the remaining freighter and the troop transport which converged on her in an attempt to ram. In the sort of manoeuvre that should only work in cartoons, *Tang* twisted out of the way at the last moment and left her two assailants to ram each other. *Tang* picked them both off with more torpedoes and made off at full speed before the escorts could intervene. So far her luck was holding.

The next day, now off Turnabout Island and still with eleven torpedoes to put to good use before he could head for home, O'Kane sighted an even larger convoy consisting of cargo ships and transports with precious aircraft stacked on their decks. Tracking them until nightfall, he again decided on a surface attack. As he approached, the Japanese ships were helpfully illuminated by the searchlights of the alert escorts and he fired a pair of torpedoes at each of three targets, destroying them all. As the water around him started erupting under gunfire from the escorts, *Tang* turned and fired three more torpedoes from her stern tubes before withdrawing to a safe distance. One hit and sank a tanker, while another crippled a transport. The third missed its intended target but may have struck a destroyer which had begun chasing the cheeky sub down (although it may have been 'friendly fire' from the other escorts which caused the destroyer to explode).

Observing this latest stroke of fortune and with his last two torpedoes left to play with, O'Kane couldn't resist turning back to finish off the crippled transport. At 900 yards, torpedo No. 23 was fired and seen to be running 'hot, straight and normal' for its target, followed shortly by No. 24. Torpedo 23 went on to sink the transport but *Tang's* luck had run out. Her final record tally of 117, 924 tons of shipping sunk included her own 1,470-ton weight. That very last torpedo, after which *Tang* could have sailed back to the safety of Pearl Harbor in triumph, travelled full circle and bit her hard in the backside. Lieutenant Commander O'Kane survived to be picked up by the Japanese and tell the tale, along with just eight others, including five men who had made a remarkable escape via the forward torpedo tubes after the submarine was settled on the seabed, 55m down.[51]

Trinidad and torpedo

USS *Tang* was not the only Second World War vessel to torpedo her-self. HMS *Trinidad*, a *Fiji*-class cruiser suffered the same indignity in March 1942, while defending an arctic convoy against German destroyers. One of the torpedoes she fired apparently did not like the icy water and tried to get back on board (though the boffins said its gyroscope was affected by the cold, making it run full circle). In this case it did not directly sink her and she managed to limp to Murmansk, escaping a U-boat attack en route, and temporary repairs were made. Great effort was then made to get her back home, with four destroyers providing close escort and a separate flotilla covering her from a distance as she crept along at reduced speed. The Luftwaffe, however, were equally keen to finish her off. Twenty Junkers Ju-88 bombers attacked her and, although only one bomb managed to hit its target, that was enough to start a serious fire in the already-damaged section, forcing her to be abandoned. To deny the Germans the satisfaction of sinking or, worse still, capturing her, *Trinidad* was then deliberately sunk by torpedoes from HMS *Matchless*.

Sunk by a brown torpedo

Being sunk by your own torpedo is embarrassing enough but spare a thought for Kapitänleutnant Karl-Adolf Schlitt, the unfortunate skipper of U-1206, who had to explain how his submarine was sunk by a blocked toilet.

A submarine is essentially a bunch of men sealed into a cramped, airtight space and going to the toilet (or 'head' in naval parlance*) in such circumstances could never be a refreshing experience at the best of times. A German type VII U-boat had just two heads between a crew of fifty men and one of these, handily positioned opposite the galley, was habitually used as an additional larder, leaving just one for its intended purpose. U-1206 was one of those lucky vessels fitted with a new improved version that could be flushed while at greater depth. However, the process for submerged flushing involved a sequence of valves that was sufficiently complicated for it to be entrusted to certain members of the crew with specialist training.

On the fateful day of 14 April 1945, while U-1206 was submerged off the Scottish coast near Peterhead, somebody decided to take advantage of these new facilities. This somebody, perhaps embarrassed by what the on-board diet of mutton and cabbage had caused them to produce, attempted to flush the toilet themselves instead of calling the specialist. It has been suggested that the skipper himself was responsible, but his own account claims he was helping with maintenance in the engine room when the problem was reported to him and that was the first he'd heard of it, honest. In any case, the result was the toilet backing up with sea water.

A leak on a submarine is never a good thing, but the new super toilet was positioned directly above the batteries, which powered the submarine when submerged. The sea water flooded into the battery compartment, the salt combining with the hydrochloric battery acid to produce chlorine gas, the same kind of gas used as a horrific weapon in the First World War. With his vessel rapidly filling with deadly fumes and water, Kapitänleutnant Schlitt had no

---

* The term 'head' comes from the age of sail, where any human waste had to be ejected from the front of the ship, adorned by the figurehead, bearing in mind that the wind is generally coming from behind a sailing vessel.

choice but to order U-1206 to surface. As the relieved crew flung open the hatches, perhaps calling the German equivalent of 'I'd give that ten minutes if I were you', they were attacked by patrolling allied aircraft. U-1206 was sunk with the loss of four men, the rest being taken prisoner.[52]

Surf 'n' turf, sushi style (Russian cow sinks Japanese fishing boat)

Following the collapse of the Soviet Union, the Russian military were not immune to the ensuing financial and administrative crisis. Various reports began to reach Western intelligence services that indicated just how bad things had got. All were no doubt received with relish and many with amusement, such as the tale of the Russian army base that had its power cut off by the electricity company for not paying their bills. Power was only restored when a tank turned up and poked its gun barrel through the company's head office door. But by far the funniest of these reports, kindly related to me by a former US Intelligence analyst, is as follows.

The Russian naval border guards answered a call for help and duly rescued some Japanese fishermen from the sea. The shaken survivors claimed that their boat had been sunk by a cow falling from the sky. Thinking this more than a little odd, the authorities launched an official investigation, which vindicated the Japanese story. In the spirit of post-Soviet entrepreneurship, some enterprising Russian Air Force aircrew had been trying to make a bit of much-needed cash by hiring out themselves and their heavy transport aircraft to carry a cargo of live cattle. The bovine passengers were duly loaded up, the plane took off happily enough and they headed out over the ocean. Unused to such cargo, however, the crew had failed to secure the cattle properly and the frightened animals, being equally unused to flying, started to panic and surge this way and that. With the aircraft becoming destabilized, the crew took the only action that made sense in such a crisis – they opened the rear ramp and tipped the cattle out into thin air. The Japanese fishing boat just happened to be in the wrong place at the wrong time and just one half-ton cow plummeting from a couple of thousand feet is plenty to make a big hole in a fishing boat.

Snake bombs

Possibly the strangest weapon to be deliberately used in ship-to-ship combat is attributed to that cunning old Carthaginian, Hannibal. After Carthage's defeat by the Romans in the Second Punic War, Hannibal was eventually forced into exile to escape Roman assassins (no one bore a grudge quite like the Romans). He headed east and offered his services to the Seleucid Empire and then to Bithynia. Although he was already a legend for his many victories over the Romans in land battles, the Bithynian king put Hannibal in charge of a fleet. In 184 BC, facing the larger fleet of Eumenes of Pergamum (a Roman proxy), the old master showed he had lost none of his flare for tactical innovation.

As the Pergamene fleet approached they were bombarded by the catapults mounted on the decks of Hannibal's ships, Eumenes' flagship being singled out for particular attention. The missiles raining down upon their decks were not the usual rocks but clay pots which smashed on impact to scatter their load of venomous, and probably rather annoyed, snakes. It is unlikely that many direct deaths from snake bites ensued, but the surprise and confusion among the ships' crews was enough to make them retreat and hand an easy victory to Hannibal.[53]

As a postscript, it was almost certainly this trick of Hannibal's that inspired a suggestion made during the Second World War to drop boxes of live snakes on Berlin, to damage enemy morale and disrupt vital war work. Not surprisingly, this idea was rejected, presumably on the reasonable grounds that venomous snakes were in short supply in Britain and ordinary high explosive bombs were a surer means to ruin a German factory worker's day.

Gullible Admiralty

In the First World War the British Admiralty gave serious consideration to a scheme to use gulls to detect enemy U-boats and give away their position by flocking around their raised periscopes. The plan was to train birds my means of dummy periscopes that dispensed food. It was eventually rejected on the grounds that the gulls would be unable to tell the difference between British and German submarines.[54]

US Navy ~~SEALS~~, dolphins and sea lions

The most exclusive unit in the US military has to be the Navy's Marine Mammals Programme, since to qualify you need to be a bottlenosed dolphin or a Californian sea lion.

The US Navy started studying marine creatures in the late 1950s and the use of dolphins and sea lions is common knowledge. In the early days, however, they also looked at sharks, rays, killer whales, beluga whales (they still have one of these) and even considered using albatrosses for locating pilots lost at sea.

Dolphins and sea lions are both currently employed for locating underwater items, notably mines but also things like training missiles, to which they can attach an acoustic marker or a recovery line if it is something the Navy wants back. Both animals are preferred to human divers because they can move faster, undertake sustained deep diving without getting the 'bends' (which can kill a human diver without the proper decompression procedures), will work for fish and have no idea how dangerous mines nor how to sue for injury. In addition, the dolphins' natural echo-location system ('biosonar') still surpasses any manmade technology at locating submerged items, particularly on the seabed; sea lions also excel at locating items underwater using acute directional hearing and phenomenal eyesight in low light and can operate in tighter or shallower spaces than a dolphin.

As well as finding and/or retrieving inanimate objects, sea lions and dolphins are also used to defend friendly vessels or installations by patrolling for intruders. They have been employed in this capacity at home in US waters and in the Middle East. An enemy diver with a bomb poses a serious threat to a modern warship at anchor. If a suspect swimmer is detected, a sea lion or dolphin can tag them with a marker and be away again before they know what is happening, leaving them for the humans to pick up or otherwise 'neutralize'. This is the officially stated procedure. There have been numerous claims that the creatures are actually trained to attack swimmers themselves. There have even been rumours that dolphins have been equipped with harnesses bearing toxic-dart guns. After Hurricane Katrina in 2005, the *Observer* newspaper (25 September 2005) reported claims that the storm had resulted in thirty-six of these marine assassins being swept out of a Louisiana coastal compound and into the Gulf of Mexico. It was feared they would be disorientated and do a Rambo, their deadly training kicking in and resulting in a rampage of darted swimmers and surfers. To allay fears, a US Navy spokesman pointed out that no such facility existed in Louisiana (the Navy keeps its seventy-five or so dolphins at San Diego, California) and that in any case dolphins don't have hands to pull triggers or press buttons to fire darts (what about voice activation?). The official website of the US Navy Marine Mammals Programme clearly states in its Frequently Asked Questions section:

> The Navy does not now train, nor has it ever trained, its marine mammals to harm or injure humans in any fashion or to carry weapons to destroy ships. .... Since dolphins cannot discern the difference between enemy and friendly vessels, or enemy and friendly divers and swimmers, it would not be wise to give that kind of decision authority to an animal. The animals are trained to detect, locate, and mark all mines or all swimmers in an area of interest or concern, and are not trained to distinguish between what we would refer to as good or bad. That decision is always left to humans.

And as they couldn't possibly have any motive for lying, that settles that, at least so far as the US is concerned.

Unfortunately it is not only the Americans that have trained dolphins for war. The Russians had a similar programme at least until the 1990s and who is to say they were as scrupulous? In 2000 no less a source than the BBC reported claims made in the Russian newspaper *Komsomolskaya Pravdarei* that ex-Soviet 'kamikaze dolphins' had been sold to Iran. These dolphins, it was claimed, had been trained by the Soviet navy for mine clearance and security patrols like their American counterparts, but also for more aggressive roles. Not only were they trained to kill enemy divers with harpoons attached to their backs but also to destroy enemy vessels with mines. Apparently more intelligent than degenerate Western dolphins, these elite operators were supposedly able to differentiate between the engine noise of enemy and friendly warships.

After the collapse of the Soviet Union, the Ukraine, hosts to the dolphins' Crimean base, didn't have the funds to sustain the program so the dolphins and their trainer, Boris Zhurid, went private. First they turned to performing circus tricks for paying audiences but civilian life didn't work out and the dolphins were in danger of starving. Like many hungry and disillusioned ex-service personnel they fell back upon what they knew best and offered their military talents to those who were prepared to pay. Lured by the promise of a bespoke new aquarium and plenty of fish, Mr Zhurid and his dolphins boarded a plane for Iran. In answer to *Komsomolskaya Pravdarei* branding him and his dolphins as mercenaries, the BBC quoted Mr Zhurid's reply as 'I am prepared to go to Allah, or even to the devil, as long as my animals will be OK there'.[55]

As I write this in early 2012 there are reports that the US is poised to send some of its dolphin teams for their third deployment to the Persian Gulf. This is in response to Iranian threats to close the strategic Straits of Hormuz, through which much of the world's oil passes, with mines. If the Iranians still have their Soviet-trained mercenary attack dolphins this opens up the prospect of dolphin-on-dolphin clashes. Are the less-aggressively trained US dolphins up to the challenge?

Chapter 12

What Do You Want – A Medal?

The Victoria Cross is Great Britain's highest military decoration, awarded for valour above and beyond the call of duty in the face of the enemy. As such it is highly prized and surrounded by a certain mystique, the proud recipients immortalized and revered as paragons of military virtue. That said, here are a few things you might find surprising or amusing.

The very first man to earn this highly prized medal, which many would give their right arm for (and some literally did), left it on a train. Charles Davis Lucas had been serving with the Royal Navy in the Crimea on 21 June 1854 when a Russian shell landed on the deck of his ship with the fuse still burning. While everyone else dived for cover, Lucas simply picked it up and tossed it overboard. When the VC was instituted two years later he was retrospectively recommended for it by his superior and received it from the Queen on 26 June 1857. To be fair, it was many years later that it was carelessly left on the train along with the other medals Lucas had by then gained. It was never recovered (if you've ever tried to get lost property back from a railway office you'll know it's probably still being used as a coaster by some moron in the office).[56]

* * *

Eight of the 1,356 VCs awarded were subsequently withdrawn from the recipients for conduct unbecoming of a hero, the associated pension also being stopped. Although there had been no such case since 1908, King George V felt the need in 1920 to recommend strongly that this token of the nation's gratitude should be for keeps, no matter what. 'Even were a VC [holder] to be sentenced to be

108

hanged for murder', the King insisted, 'he should be allowed to wear his VC on the scaffold'.

* * *

Only one VC has been awarded to a man who directly nominated himself. The heroic deed for which Major William Knox Leet was so pleased with himself occurred during the Anglo-Zulu War. To be precise it was at the battle of Mount Hlobane on 28 March 1879 that Major Leet paused during a rapid tactical withdrawal (some would say ignominious flight) to help another fleeing officer onto his own horse and thus back to safety. The grateful officer did praise Leet's action in his post-action report and this was forwarded to Leet's commanding officer, Colonel Wood, himself already a VC holder. Wood in turn duly mentioned it in reports to his seniors but there was no actual recommendation of an award so Leet took matters into his own hands. He wrote a letter to a family friend of his, a Colonel Goldsworthy in which he wrote:

> They all say here that I ought to get the VC for saving young Smith's life at the risk of my own, but Col. Wood being a VC man himself (I do not know with what foundation) does not care to increase the number more than he can help. ... Do you think I deserve it? If so, can you assist me in this matter? You have connections with the Press, and in that way (of course without compromising me in any way) you might bring public opinion to bear. ... I would give my eyes for a VC if outsiders think I deserve it ... I hope the general is quite well, remember me most kindly to him.[57]

Perhaps if Leet had known how Colonel (later Field Marshal) Evelyn Wood had earned his VC, he might have shown more respect and, perhaps, just a little more humility. In 1856 the then Captain Wood had led the grenadier company of the 20th Bengal Native Infantry over the parapets of an enemy fort during the Persian War. He was shot seven times in the process but still carried on to personally run the Persian commander through with his sword.[58] It is understandable that he wasn't more impressed with Leet's feat of helping another chap to run away while running away himself. Anyway,

Leet's string-pulling worked and he was awarded the coveted medal.

* * *

By contrast with Leet's self-promotion, two recipients gained their VCs on the recommendation of the enemy. Both performed their heroics at sea during the Second World War. The first went to Lieutenant Commander Gerard Broadmeade Roope, skipper of the destroyer HMS *Glowworm*. On 8 April 1940 Roope spotted two German destroyers escorting troopships en route to invade Norway and, thinking nothing of two-to-one odds, he immediately attacked. The Germans attempted to disengage and radioed for reinforcements in the form of the heavy cruiser *Admiral Hipper*, a vastly more powerful ship, which was nearby and happy to oblige.

To say *Glowworm* had bitten off more than she could chew is something of an understatement. *Glowworm*, displacing a modest 1,370 tons, was armed with two torpedo tubes and four 4-inch guns, while the 16,000-ton *Hipper* had eight much heavier 8-inch guns that could outrange her opponent as well as twelve 4.1-inch guns and six torpedo tubes. *Hipper*'s big guns soon found their mark and *Glowworm* started taking a pounding. Now it was Roope's turn to attempt a tactical withdrawal under cover of a smoke screen but *Hipper*'s radar-directed guns were unaffected, so Roope counter-attacked by doubling back and firing off five torpedoes. All of these missed and one of the tubes jammed, while *Glowworm* sustained terrible damage to her bridge, engine rooms and forward guns. Seeing *Glowworm* again retreating through her own smoke, the *Hipper*'s skipper, Kapitän Hellmuth Heye ordered his ship to follow, closing in to finish her off before she could fire her remaining torpedoes.

But Roope wasn't yet done with *Hipper*. Heye must have been astonished to see the British destroyer suddenly loom back out of the smoke, siren wailing and heading straight for him. He ordered evasive action but the big ship was too slow and *Glowworm* rammed her, breaking off her own bow and gouging a huge gash in the cruiser's armoured flank before drifting away, a blazing wreck. *Glowworm*'s boilers exploded shortly after and what was left of her went down. Heye stopped to pick up survivors, saving forty, but as the exhausted Roope was being hauled up the cruiser's side he fell back into the sea and drowned. Even though it turned out that *Glowworm*'s ramming tactics were almost certainly accidental (her rudder had been smashed and her emergency rudder was unmanned – the nice touch of the wailing siren was also the result of damage rather than defiance), the destroyer's fighting spirit had so impressed Heye that he wrote to the British Admiralty describing the action and suggesting that they give her plucky commander the highest possible decoration. Roope's VC was the first of the Second World War.[59]

While *Kapitän* Heye's glowing report was obviously a big part in Roope's award, there were British survivors to corroborate and support his recommendation of a decoration. This was not so in Flying Officer Lloyd Trigg's case. Trigg was one of many men of the Royal New Zealand Air Force who served far from home in British RAF squadrons, in this case 200 Squadron, stationed in West Africa. On 11 August 1943 he was flying a patrol off the coast near Bathurst in a B-24 Liberator bomber (serial no. BZ832 to be precise). Spotting a German submarine on the surface, he attacked. The crew of the submarine, *U-468*, were alert and opened an accurate fire with their anti-aircraft guns. Trigg's plane was repeatedly hit and set ablaze but he continued his attacks, dropping six depth charges from a height of less than 50 feet. The German gunners reported actually being able to see their shells striking inside the open bomb bay, so low and slow was the plane's final pass. The Liberator then plunged into the sea, killing Trigg and the other seven men of his crew but the depth charges did their work, destroying the U-boat. Many of *U-468*'s fifty-one crewmen went down with their vessel and most of the remainder succumbed to wounds, drowned or were eaten by sharks in the next two days, before an Allied ship arrived to pick up the last survivors. These consisted of the U-boat's commander, Oberleutnant Klemens Schamong, and just six others who had ironically been saved by an inflatable dinghy from the wreckage of Trigg's aircraft. Despite their ordeal they spoke so highly of their courage of their adversary that Trigg posthumously received the only VC awarded solely on the enemy's testimony.[60]

* * *

Several Victoria Crosses were won by mere boys of only fifteen or sixteen years of age, with three examples coming from the 1857 Indian Mutiny alone. Sixteen-year-old Bugler Robert Hawthorn was with the 'explosion party' that blasted its way into Lucknow to relieve the garrison and braved heavy fire to drag his wounded officer to safety. Also at Lucknow, Bandboy George Monger of the 23rd Foot similarly risked his life to save a wounded man caught in crossfire, in this case laying himself over a wounded corporal as a human shield.[61] Drummer Thomas Flynn of the 64th Foot took a more aggressive approach. Already wounded, he charged an enemy cannon and single-handedly overcame two of the gunners in hand-to-hand combat. He was fifteen years old. Two days after receiving his VC from a grateful Queen, Flynn was still celebrating and was imprisoned for drunkenness. His military career went downhill from there and he was repeatedly disciplined for various offences until he left the army in 1869. This true Victorian hero died in a workhouse in 1892.[62]

Thousands of boys served in the British Army, mainly as drummers and buglers, a vital role in battlefield command and control before the days of radios. Many were the product of army asylums – military schools for the orphans of soldiers. Others were the sons of men still serving, 'born into the regiment' and enlisted as soon as they were deemed old enough to be useful. Probably the youngest was Drummer James Wade of the 95th Foot whose army career began on his seventh birthday! Remarkably, there was no minimum age for enlistment in the British Army until namby-pamby liberal thinking in the 1880s resulted in the lower limit being set at the ripe old age of fourteen.[63]

Chapter 13

Undiplomatic Responses

Diplomacy goes hand in hand with warfare. Before committing their young men to harm's way, even the most callow dictators will often attempt to gain victory by diplomacy first. Even the boldest generals will offer the enemy a chance to surrender to avoid unnecessary bloodshed on both sides. Sometimes, however, even when the logic of the situation suggests that eating humble pie or even total surrender is the most rational answer, the response is decidedly undiplomatic.

Earth and water

Darius, Persian King of Kings, was not a man used to being defied. From Libya in the West to Afghanistan and Pakistan in the East his word was law. Millions of subjects (over 40 per cent of the world's population at the time, it is estimated) paid their taxes to him, hailed him as their lord and master and tried not to come to the attention of 'the King's eyes', his network of spies and enforcers. The ruins of Persian palaces still bear reliefs showing ambassadors in a varied array of distinctive ethnic costumes queuing to prostrate themselves at the feet of the king and offer earth and water, the traditional tokens of submission. In modern parlance, he was the daddy.

So, when some of the Greek-speaking cities of Ionia (Western Asia Minor, the Aegean coast of modern Turkey) started rebelling against his rule in 499 BC, he was not amused to learn that they had been encouraged and even actively assisted in their insolence by some insignificant little cities in mainland Greece, beyond his borders (i.e. he had not got round to conquering it yet). The chief culprit was Athens, which we now look to as the founder of Western culture but which Darius had probably scarcely heard of. From then on he heard of it every day, having commanded one of his many servants

113

to whisper 'Master, remember the Athenians' into his ear three times at every meal, lest he forget to punish them. By 493 BC he had crushed the rebellion in Ionia and, like the eye of Sauron, turned his furious gaze west. Deciding he might as well teach the Athenians a lesson and bring the rest of Greece to appreciate the benefit of his rule at the same time, he sent his victorious generals westward to overrun Thrace (roughly modern Romania) and Macedonia while he started gathering a fresh army and an unprecedented armada of 600 ships to carry them and their supplies. At the same time he sent ambassadors to the cities of Greece to demand their surrender.

Now, consider that Darius' elite bodyguard unit alone numbered 10,000 men and that this turned out to be the maximum number of fully-armed men that Athens or Sparta, the two main powers in Greece, could field at a real pinch and you should understand that Darius had every reason to expect to get what he wanted with, at most, a show of strength. His ambassadors were used to being greeted by cowering, fawning potentates who handed over the required tokens and begged the Great King's mercy. Indeed, this is exactly the response they found in many of the Greek cities, but, when they got to Athens they were put on trial in front of the democratic mob and executed. The Spartans were equally defiant but accomplished it with more wit. When the Persian diplomats asked for earth and water, the symbolic tokens of submission, they were chucked down a deep well and told they would find plenty of both at the bottom.

Laconic comics

The Spartans, as well as being hard-as-nails psychopaths, were masters at this kind of concise wit. Sparta was the city, the region it sat in was Lakonia and it is from this that we get the word 'laconic', used to describe speech that hits the nail on the head with few words. Darius' son, Xerxes, was to provoke a further couple of classic examples of laconic diplomatic wit.

In 490 BC, stung by the barbaric maltreatment of ambassadors described above, Darius' huge army was shipped across to Greece, conquering many of the Aegean islands en route, to finally trample the pesky Athenians into the dirt. Unfortunately, the much smaller

Athenian army had not read the script and trounced his army at the Battle of Marathon, forcing the Persian forces to withdraw ignominiously. Distracted by a rebellion in Egypt, Darius had still not settled the score before he died. So, along with his vast empire, Xerxes inherited from Darius a massive grudge against the Greeks.

Intent on avenging his father's humiliation, in 480 BC Xerxes mustered an even more immense army drawn from many far-flung corners of his realm. Among its exotic ranks it included camel-riding Arabs, swarthy Indians in chariots, lasso-twirling Sargatian horsemen from the central Asian steppes who virtually lived in their saddles, Ethiopians who painted one half of themselves vermillion and chalked the other white – though sadly none of the rhinoceroses that appeared in the movie version, *300*. This was an army so enormous that it reportedly drank rivers dry as it tramped westward along the coast of Thrace, shadowed offshore by the largest fleet any man had ever laid eyes on. When the expedition reached a point where part of his father's fleet had been wrecked rounding a particular headland, Xerxes simply had his army dig a canal right across the peninsula. Cut through 1.5 miles of rock, it was wide enough for two ships to pass abreast. Geography itself could not defy the King of Kings.

Now it must be remembered that Greece at this time was not a unified country, just a bunch of independent cities whose shared ties of language, culture and religion did nothing to stop them spending most of their time either at war with each other, or preparing to go to war with each other. Most would not rate as cities at all today. Athens, the largest city, had only managed to muster about 10,000 fully-armed infantry (hoplites) for the crucial fight at Marathon. Sparta, already acknowledged as the most formidable military power in Greece, would only manage to field 10,000 hoplites at full stretch, of which only half were full-blown Spartan citizens. Even if all the Greeks had banded together in an uncharacteristic fit of cooperation, they would not have been able to match the might of the Persians assembled to bear down on them.

At the narrow pass of Thermopylai this vast Persian horde found its way blocked by a Greek force of about 10,000, led by the Spartan king Leonidas and his little contingent of just 300 Spartans (think

Gerard Butler and co. but with armour instead of just leather Speedos). Darius sent envoys to demand their surrender. When the offer of terms was refused, the envoys reminded the Greeks that Xerxes' archers were so numerous that their arrows would block out the sun. 'Good', replied a Spartan, 'then we shall fight in the shade'.

The Persian army battered itself against the Greek defences for several days, before a local Greek showed them a route by which they could outflank the defenders. Leonidas sent away most of the Greek allies, keeping only 300 of his Spartans to delay the inevitable as long as possible by a defiant last stand. Xerxes, impressed by the Spartans' courage, decided to offer them one last chance to live. He sent an envoy demanding that the Spartans surrender their weapons. The message he received back from Leonidas simply said 'come and get them'.

The Spartans, of course died to a man, but their defiance won them immortal fame.

If

Philip II of Macedon, though best remembered as the father of Alexander the Great (think Val Kilmer's dodgy beard to Colin Farrell's badly bleached Alexander in the 2004 movie version), was a mighty warlord in his own right. While he was involved in the Third Sacred War of 346 BC, Philip was keen to keep the Spartans from coming in on the side of his enemies, so he sent a message warning that if he decided to bring his army to their lands they were in big trouble. The reply was just a single word, one of his own thrown back at him: 'if'.

After gently persuading most of the Greek city-states to join an alliance under his leadership, by crushing the major players in battle, he again turned his attention to the Spartans. Hoping to intimidate them by a show of force, he marched his formidable army towards their borders, sending a message ahead to ask whether he should enter Spartan territory as a friend or as an enemy. Again the reply, according to Plutarch, was just one word: 'neither'.[64] Philip never did tackle the insolent Spartans and nor, amazingly, did his seemingly-invincible son. Macedonian policy thereafter was effectively to pretend they never really wanted the Spartans to join their gang anyway and really teaching them a lesson by going off to conquer the Persian Empire without them.

The winds of war

When the Egyptian pharaoh Apries (reigned 589–570 BC) sent an army to invade Libya, it went so disastrously wrong that the survivors who made it back raised a rebellion against him. Apries sent Amasis to 'argue the rebels into submission' but, while he was 'doing his best to persuade them to return to their duty' one of the rebels came up behind him, placed a helmet on his head and proclaimed him king. According to Herodotus' account 'Amasis was not altogether displeased with this' and prepared to lead them against Apries.

Apries soon got wind of this danger, literally. He 'sent Patarbemis, a distinguished member of his court, to bring Amasis alive into his presence'. This august dignitary duly sought out the rebel and told him he had come to take him in. Herodotus relates his response thus:

> Amasis, however, in answer to Patarbemis' summons, rose in his saddle (he was on horseback at the time), broke wind and told him to take *that* back to his master.
>
> [Herodotus, *Histories*, II.162]

When the unfortunate Patarbemis returned with this less than diplomatic response, Apries was so incensed that he had his nose and ears cut off. The outrage to the distinguished and loyal Patarbemis was the catalyst for a general uprising and most of the country went over to the rebels. Apries confronted the usurper's army with a force composed of foreign mercenaries but was defeated and captured. Amasis (now pharaoh and known as Ahmose II) was inclined to mercy and let his former monarch live in comfortable captivity in a palace but the ordinary Egyptians later lynched and strangled him, though they did bury him properly in his family tomb.

Defiance in a word

In December of 1944, when the Germans made their last great counterattack through the snow-clad Ardennes, they completely surprised the worn-out American units that had been sent to this 'quiet sector' to rest and recuperate. The Germans initially swept all before them but encountered a stubborn pocket of defenders around the little town of Bastogne. The self-styled 'Battered Bastards of Bastogne' held off all attacks against incredible odds. Surrounding them with masses of armoured formations and battle-hardened infantry, the Germans called upon them to surrender or be annihilated. The reply that came back from the American commander, Major General McAuliffe was a single word – 'Nuts!'

The 'Bastards' held out until reinforcements of Patton's Third Army arrived and halted the German offensive, spoiling Hitler's last great gamble for victory in the West.

Hitting the nail on the head

Vladimir III, who ruled the principality of Wallachia on and off in the mid-fifteenth century, was constantly at war with the Ottoman Turks. When Sultan Mehmet II sent two ambassadors to talk peace they probably approached with some trepidation since the prince already had a reputation for a bad temper and sadistic cruelty. Better known to history as Vlad the Impaler after his favourite form of execution (sometimes whole crowds of prisoners were herded over the edge of spiked pits), he bore the surname Dracula (being the son of Vlad Dracul) and much later inspired the name of Bram Stoker's famous bloodthirsty character*.

Still, the Turkish ambassadors were representing arguably the most powerful man in the world at this time and could therefore expect to be treated with some respect by this minor prince. When they were admitted to Vlad's presence, however, they approached him with their heads covered by turbans. Vlad, who was used to much bowing, scraping and doffing of caps, took this as a grave insult and insisted they remove their headgear. When the ambassadors refused, their turbans being a mark of their Muslim faith after all, Vlad decided to make sure they would never remove them

* Apparently Stoker's character was originally going to be called Count Wampyr and the book was already nearly finished when he strayed across the historical Dracula and Transylvania (though of course Vlad was from neighbouring Wallachia), thought they sounded good and wrote them in.

for anyone else either. On his order the unfortunate Turks were seized and their turbans fixed permanently to their heads with long nails hammered through into their skulls. Needless to say the war with the Turks went on.

Counting the days

At the siege of Maastricht in 1676 a German nobleman in the besieging Allied army sent a cheeky message to the defending Spanish governor, Count Calvo, saying that he looked forward to kissing the hand of the the governor's mistress inside the city within three weeks. A confident Count Calvo replied that he would give him permission to kiss the lady all over if he kissed her anywhere inside of three weeks.[65]

Sticky end for Napoleon's Old Guard

In the late afternoon of the fateful day of 18 July 1815, the Battle of Waterloo was entering its final phase. Three battalions of Napoleon's elite, the Old Guard, who had sealed so many of his victories, now found themselves surrounded as the rest of the French army crumbled away around them in defeat. The British called upon the Guards' commander, General Crambonne, to avoid needless bloodshed and surrender. Determined to stand by his emperor to the end (never mind that the little Corsican was already making use of his getaway carriage), Crambonne gave are heroic reply befitting the epic occasion. The sources, however, are divided on exactly what he said. Some accounts give the elegant rejoinder: 'The Guard dies but it does not surrender!' Others give the more pithy, but equally defiant 'Merde!' The General and all his men were cut down in a hail of musket balls and grapeshot.

Chapter 14

The Pressures of High Command

Spartan king goes to pieces

Cleomenes I of Sparta was a veteran campaigner with a proven track record of being ruthless and effective when he started to behave somewhat erratically. Herodotus explains that he had always 'been a little strange in the head' but now completely lost the plot, wandering round Sparta, jabbing every citizen he met in the face with his staff. In Sparta, no one was above the law and, king or not, this sort of thing could not be tolerated for long. His own family had him restrained with his legs in the stocks. He persuaded the slave left to keep an eye on him, through threats of the terrible things he would do once he got out of there, to give him a knife. Herodotus explains what happened next:

> As soon as the knife was in his hands, Cleomenes began to mutilate himself, beginning on his shins. He sliced his flesh into strips, working upwards to his thighs, and from there to his hips and sides, until he reached his belly, and while he was cutting that into strips he died. [Herodotus, VI.75]

Some of his contemporaries saw Cleomenes' madness as divine retribution for his actions in campaigns against the Argives, where he had broken oaths, burnt down a sacred grove where defeated enemy had taken cover, killed the odd priest and generally not played nicely. Others attributed it to the heavy drinking habit he had picked up from the wild Scythians while campaigning in their lands.

Justin II – Roman emperor *à la cart*

Being commander-in-chief of all Rome's vaunted military forces was never an easy task. After the disastrous battle of the Teutoberg

Forest in 9 AD, the Emperor Augustus famously had a spell of banging his head on the palace walls and crying 'bring me back my legions'. This is nothing to what the pressures of the job did to Justin II. By the sixth century AD the western half of the mighty Roman Empire had been overrun and divvied up between various tribes of hairy Germanic barbarians, leaving the Eastern half centred on Constantinople (aka the Byzantine Empire) to fight on alone. Justin II, who reigned from AD 565 to 578, was so upset by the loss of the city of Dara to the Persians that he went completely bonkers. According to John of Ephesus, 'he even uttered the cries of various animals, and barked like a dog, and bleated like a goat; and then he would mew like a cat, and then again crow like a cock'. Often he would be filled 'with agitation and terror, so that he rushed about in furious haste from place to place' as if pursued, sometimes hiding beneath his bed or trying to leap from the windows. All the windows on one side of the imperial palace had to be barred and strong men appointed to be his 'chamberlains'. When they tried to restrain poor Justin, he would turn on them and bite them savagely, on one occasion mauling two men so severely about the head that they were incapacitated and a rumour spread through the imperial city that the emperor had eaten them.

As Justin was completely off his metaphorical trolley, his servants built him a real one complete with a throne, in which they would push the gibbering emperor around his palace at speed to keep him amused. To add to the surreal atmosphere, organ music was found to be the surest way to calm his tortured mind and so was played day and night. This still did not stop him having the terrors or less dark episodes, such as the time he was found at a palace window shouting 'who will buy my lovely pots and pans'. And so it went on for the last five years of his life.

Field Marshal Blücher – a very senior officer

This redoubtable old warrior was already in his seventies when he had his finest hour, arriving at the head of his Prussian army to save the British and seal Napoleon's fate at the Battle of Waterloo in June 1815. He was already barking mad too. Apparently he had the recurring delusion that he was pregnant with a baby elephant. That would have been bad enough, but this unwanted offspring would not even have a decent suitable father, since Blücher was convinced that it was a lowly soldier, and one of the hated French enemy to boot, that had somehow knocked him up.

Charles VI shattered by knight dropping a clanger

Being 'King of the French' during the Hundred Years War was not an easy gig, what with English armies marching across your land and all that, but Charles VI took the stress of the job particularly badly. I doubt it helped that he was saddled with the job in 1380, when he was just eleven years old. By July 1392, Charles had grown into his crown and was leading an army into Brittany to punish the Duke of Brittany for harbouring a man who had attempted to kill a friend of the king.

As the army advanced along a forest road in potentially hostile territory, the king was naturally a bit on edge, the more so after some ragged old loon ran up and warned him to turn back as treachery was afoot. But when one of his knights dropped his lance and it clanged noisily against a helmet, the king completely flipped out. Imagining himself under attack, he drew his sword and started laying about him, killing at least one of his escort and injuring others before he could be restrained.

Although this episode soon passed, the king's mind had been unhinged. This was just the first of the numerous bouts of insanity, during which his uncles would squabble over who was running the shop, and it is not surprising the war with the English went badly for the rest of his reign. Like Justin II (above) he sometimes ran frantically around his palace, doors and windows having to be blocked up for his own protection. On occasions he did not recognize his own family and thought his own name was George. By the time poor Charles '*le Fou*' (Charles 'the Mad'), as he came to be known, faced England's Henry V at the Battle of Agincourt, he was suffering delusions that he was made of glass and would strike out at his entourage to prevent them touching and shattering him.

Chapter 15

Miscellaneous

Last-man standing

Around 550 BC, the Spartans, who were the original neighbours from hell, marched over the border with neighbouring Argos and occupied land around a town called Thyreae. The Argives, understandably peeved, mustered their army and marched to Thyreae to reclaim their land. Instead of immediately setting about each other in full force, however, negotiations produced a plan to settle the dispute while limiting the damage. Each side was to select 300 men to fight it out in what was effectively a mass duel. To ensure neither side attempted to intervene if its side was losing, the two main armies were to march away and leave them to it, then reconvene for the post-match analysis the following day. Thyreae would go to the side whose representatives had won the fight. Simple as that.

Both armies picked their best team, marched off and the combat, known as the Battle of Champions, kicked off as planned. The heroic champions battled hard all day but were so closely matched that only two Argives and one Spartan were left alive when nightfall put an end to proceedings. The Argives, Alcenor and Chromios, promptly set off for home to tell of their 2-1 home win. The lone Spartan, Othryades, remained on the field long enough to strip the Argive dead of their armour and carry some of it back to the Spartan camp, it being the traditional act of a victorious army to take captured equipment as victory trophies.

When the two armies met up again the next day, both were claiming victory, the Argives on the grounds that more of their champions had survived, the Spartans on the basis that the last Argives had quit the field of battle. Neither side was inclined to back down and the quarrel got more and more heated, eventually erupting into the precisely the kind of full-blown battle between the main armies that they had been trying to avoid. This time the Spartans emerged as clear victors but only after both sides had suffered severe losses.

The Argives were so furious at the loss of Thyreae that they passed a law that compelled all the city's men, who customarily wore their hair long, to cut it short, and forbade all women to wear gold, until the lost territory was regained. According to Herodotus it was in direct response to this that Spartan men, having hitherto kept their hair short, chose to grow theirs in the long locks for which they are famous. Othryades, apparently, was so ashamed at having out-lived the 299 colleagues who died a brave death in the first fight that he refused to return to Sparta and committed suicide.[66]

It's good to talk

Just occasionally, even in the heat of battle, men can talk and settle things amicably without all the usual unpleasantness. At the Battle of Dresden, 27 August 1813, a French heavy cavalry division led by General Bourdesoule approached an Austrian infantry brigade. They approached slowly as it was raining heavily and the fields had turned to mud. Bourdesoule, noting the lack of defensive fire coming from the enemy formation, rode up and invited the Austrian commander to surrender on the grounds that his men's muskets would clearly not work in the wet conditions.* The Austrian officer politely declined on the grounds that the heavy mud, which was up to the horse's hocks, would equally clearly prevent the French cavalry charging effectively. Bourdesoule considered this thought-ful response for a moment before trumping it by saying he would bring up some artillery, so they really should surrender. The Austrian was unimpressed and again refused to surrender, this time giving the reason that cannon could surely not be hauled through such mud any time soon. It was only when the French, having had the foresight to allocate extra horses to their artillery teams, unlim-bered a couple of cannon just 30 yards away that the Austrian con-ceded the argument and surrendered.[67]

* Flintlock muskets were vulnerable to damp because they had be primed with dry gunpowder, hence the phrase 'keep your powder dry', meaning to save something (money, a clever comment?) for when it will be really useful.

Nina versus the Nazis

On 22 June 1941 German forces invaded the Soviet Union, sweeping before them the totally surprised Russians who had been their allies up to that point. With German panzers rapidly closing in on Moscow, Stalin and his cronies started making plans to abandon their capital. Intending to keep up the fight even if the city fell, however, they put plans in place for a resistance movement to make things tricky for the German occupiers (following in the tradition of denying the city to Napoleon by torching it in 1812).

One devilish scheme they came up with was to train a group of four theatre performers for a special mission. If the Germans took the city, they were to ingratiate themselves with the occupiers and get themselves invited to perform at the celebratory concert it was assumed they would through for all their victorious generals. It was hoped Hitler himself might even attend. When the others (a tune whistler, a guy who wrote funny sketches and a singer) had done their parts, Nina the Juggler was to take the stage for the grand finale. At the right moment she was to lob her juggling skittles, which were of course pre-packed with high explosives, into the assembled Nazi top brass and win the war (if not much immediate applause). What could possibly go wrong? Nina and the rest of the troupe were said to be both disappointed and a little relieved when the Red Army (and 'General Winter') halted the Nazis outside Moscow and the show was indefinitely postponed.[68]

Chapter 16

Weird and Wonderful Weapons

Throughout history, mankind has poured vast amounts of energy and ingenuity into inventing more effective, more efficient, or sometimes just more spectacular ways of killing each other. Of the following selection, some worked, some failed, some never got off the drawing board and others are just about to.

Swing low sweet chariot

One of the least successful weapon systems of all time has to be the scythed chariot. Most of the armies of the great early civilizations of the Mediterranean and Middle East used regular chariots successfully for hundreds of years from the mid-second millenium BC. They formed the elite of the armies of the Egyptians, Assyrians, Hittites and the like. A driver managed the horses (2hp or 4hp versions were available), acting as chauffeur for a noble warrior, usually with a bow and arrows as his primary weapons, who got to have the actual fun of smiting the enemy in what amounted to a series of drive-by shootings. But the scythed variant didn't appear until the fifth century BC, by which time ordinary chariots had been rendered obsolete and replaced in most armies by cavalry (i.e. warriors actually riding *on* horses) which were cheaper, more manoeuvrable and better at handling rough terrain*.

*The classic illustration of this is Alexander the Great's battle against an Indian army at the River Hydaspes in 326 BC. The Indians were still using chariots in large numbers, though they fielded even larger numbers of cavalry. When Alexander's cavalry led an outflanking manouevre across the river, it was met by a force of chariots but these were easily defeated as their wheels became stuck in the muddy ground.

We cannot be certain which genius suggested that all that the chariot really needed by way of a revamp was to stick some long, sharp blades on the wheel hubs, but the first reliably recorded instance of their use is at the Battle of Cunaxa in 401 BC. There the Persian Prince Cyrus led a rebel army bolstered with Greek mercenary infantry against the Persian king, his brother. According to the eyewitness account of Xenophon, one of the Greek mercenaries, there were fifty of these contraptions spaced out in front of the king's battle line.

This was not the most sophisticated weapon system. The idea was simply to drive the chariots through enemy formations so that the whirring blades could carve up anyone who didn't get clear in time and terrify the rest. Unlike regular chariots they seem only to have carried one man, and as the job was pretty much suicidal you can be fairly sure they were not drawn from the nobility. But at Cunaxa the Greeks did not timidly wait to be driven into, instead launching a vigorous but disciplined attack that caused most of the Persians to flee before they even got close and the chariots simply added to the confusion:

> The chariots rushed about, some going through the enemy's own ranks, though some, abandoned by their drivers, did go through the Greeks. When they saw them coming the Greeks opened out, though one man stood rooted to the spot, as though he was at a race course, and got run down. However, even he, they said, came to no harm.[69]

Despite this disastrous debut the scythed chariot was not consigned to the dustbin of history and it was resurrected by Persian and other rulers in this general region several times over the next few centuries – usually with similar results. When the Persian King of Kings, Darius III, gathered all his remaining forces to try to halt Alexander the Great at the Battle of Gaugamela (332 BC) he had 200 scythed chariots. Again these were strung out in front of the Persian battle line, where their charge would hopefully break up the enemy formations. Fifty of them were posted opposite Alexander's own position amid his elite cavalry, the Companions, but he responded by putting a screen of light infantry with bows and javelins in between. According to Arrian:

the chariots were no sooner off the mark than they were met by the missile weapons of the Agrianes and Balacrus' javelin throwers, who were stationed in advance of the Companions; again they seized the reins and dragged the drivers to the ground, then surrounded the horses and cut them down.[70]

The few that broke through the loose formation of the light infantry were met coolly by the Companions who opened gaps in their ranks, through which the terrified chariot horses naturally galloped, only to be rounded up in the rear once they had run out of steam by the young grooms that served the Companions. One account of the battle does suggest the scythed chariots further down the line inflicted some damage on Alexander's infantry and takes delight in describing how they left 'the ground littered with the severed limbs of the soldiers'. But if this was not merely a literary flourish it was most likely a very localized (and short-lived) success by the few chariots that made it through to the Macedonian second line. Most were skewered from either side by the infantrymen's pikes as they again careered down channels opened in the disciplined phalanx formation.

You might expect that the Seleucid kings, the ethnic Macedonian dynasty that ruled much of the former Persian Empire after Alexander's death, might have known better. But they again revived the scythed chariot for use against the Romans in the early second century BC. At the crucial Battle of Magnesia the scythed chariots did indeed manage to cut swathes through dense formations and cause a panicked rout, but as these formations were on their own side it was not exactly the desired effect.

Still in the same region but about a century later, King Mithridates VI of Pontus (part of modern Turkey near the Black Sea) also decided to give these death traps a go. To be fair, though details are lacking, they do seem to have played a large part in one of his early victories against the neighbouring Bithynians and their Roman allies. But when he came up against disciplined Roman legions at Chaeronea they, like the Greeks at Cunaxa, counterattacked his ninety-four scythed chariots before they had really got going. They were defeated with such ease that the Roman infantry laughed and clapped and called out 'bring on more!', as if they were at the Circus.

Despite their terrible combat record, it is easy to see the appeal of the scythed chariot – who would not be tempted by a speeding vehicle with flashing blades on the wheels? They do, after all, look fantastic in films like *Gladiator*. Although there is no evidence that the Romans actually adopted them, the *De Rebus Bellicus*, a sort of catalogue of military boys' toys, does show a souped up version with a heavily armoured warrior mounted on each horse and folding scythes. As late as the fifteenth century, that forward-thinking genius Leonardo da Vinci even reinvented it all over again!

Ironically, the person arguably most associated with the scythed chariot in the minds of the general public (in Britain at least) probably never even saw one. The statue by London's Westminster Bridge notwithstanding, there is no evidence that Boudicca (or Boadicea if you prefer the now-unfashionable Victorian spelling) had scythes on her chariot when she rebelled against Roman rule. Although the British were backward enough to be using regular chariots on the battlefield against Julius Caesar's abortive invasions in the first century BC, there was no mention in his accounts of scythed wheels. By the time of the successful invasion in AD 43 even the regular variety seem to have finally fallen out of fashion, though some were used in the far north as late as the Battle of Mons Graupius in AD 84.

Far to the east in China, the chariot remained in use alongside cavalry much longer. They do not appear to have employed the scythed chariot but, faced with the same problem of breaking up dense enemy formations, one general seems to have come up with something even more remarkable. Around AD 180, the Han general Yang Hsuan faced a battle against vastly more numerous rebel forces. Necessity being the mother of invention, he came up with what was perhaps the world's first (deliberately) unmanned fighting vehicle.

The driver could be dispensed with as the chariot was only required to make a single run straight toward the enemy. To make sure the horses kept going full speed, their tails were set alight.

Stampeding, blazing horses dragging rumbling contraptions behind them might have been enough to unnerve the rebels, especially as the Han had already half blinded them by releasing sackloads of lime dust to blow downwind towards them, but Yang was taking no chances. The chariots were unmanned but they were not unarmed. Mounted on each chariot were multiple crossbows, angled to fire forward and obliquely to both flanks. The triggers were connected to cords that were fixed to the chariot's axle. As the chariots careered forward, the turning of the wheels wound the cords tighter about the axle, eventually pulling the triggers and firing volleys of crossbow bolts into the bewildered ranks of the enemy. By the time Yang's men reached them the rebels were already half beaten and easily defeated.[71]

A soldier's best friend is his rifle ... sometimes

When Canada sent its Expeditionary Force of about 30,000 men off to Europe to fight in the First World War they were armed with the Ross Rifle. There was nothing particularly revolutionary about it and it was a little long and heavy compared to rival designs but trials had shown it to be an accurate target rifle. Of course it didn't hurt that Sam Hughes, the Minister for the Militia and Defence responsible for awarding the $80,000 contract, was a friend of Charles Ross, the rifle's inventor.

There was just one minor drawback to the Ross Rifle that emerged once it reached the Western Front – it was particularly prone to jamming in muddy conditions and there was more than a little mud about. It didn't help that the Canadians were issued with British ammunition which, though nominally of the same .303-inch calibre, varied slightly, while the Ross was very precisely manufactured and fussy about its ammunition. The bolt mechanism, used to eject spent cartridges and load another round from the magazine for firing, would expand with the hot gases produced in firing and jam after a few shots, sticking fast until it cooled down again. Soldiers in action around Ypres resorted to stomping on the bolts with their muddy boots to shift them, getting more mud in the mechanism. If this were not inconvenient enough when a horde of 'the Hun' was coming over the hill, the Ross would occasionally do its special party trick of launching its firing bolt back into the aiming eye of the firer. Not surprisingly, it is regarded by many as the worst rifle ever issued to an army. Eventually, in 1916, the Ross was replaced with British rifles and the scandal led to the resignation of Sam Hughes, the cancellation of further orders (30,000 of the Mark III alone had already been bought) and the closure of the Ross factory.

The Tsar Tank

The British were the first to use tanks in action, during the later stages of the infamous Battle of the Somme in 1916, coming as a real surprise to the Germans. However, others had been working along similar lines in other countries for some time. Armoured vehicles in the form of armoured cars were in use by most of the major participants at the outbreak of war, but these generally carried only a machine gun or two and had limited off-road performance, essentially being motor cars (themselves still a fairly new invention of course) weighed down with armour plating. What engineers and forward-thinking generals on both sides wanted was a big machine with big guns to blast stuff out of its path and simply roll over anything that was left of the enemy, trenches, barbed wire and all.

As early as 1914, a group of Russian engineers was already working on producing such a wonder weapon. What they came up with looked very different to the British tanks. Instead of tracks it had a pair of huge wheels, 27 feet in diameter, each powered by a 250hp engine. These wheels were joined by an axle and set, by means of robust armoured arms, in front of a 40-feet-wide superstructure with a main gun turret in the centre and sponsons carrying further cannon projecting at either side. Behind this superstructure trailed a third wheel so the whole thing looked like a sort of armoured tricycle in reverse. The giant front wheels were for rolling over obstacles, while the rear wheel, to assist steering, was much smaller, about 5 feet in diameter. In profile it looked like one of those Victorian penny-farthing bikes.

The appearance of such a towering machine would no doubt have caused at least as much panic among the Germans as the relatively low and compact British tanks did in 1916, though the huge wheels, which had rather spindly spokes just like a bicycle, would have been very vulnerable to artillery fire. It remains a moot point since the Tsar Tank never got into action. When the prototype was tested in front of assembled top brass in August 1915, the front wheels did their job of rolling over obstacles but the puny back wheel got stuck in a ditch and refused to budge. And there the stranded beast remained for the next eight years until it was finally dismantled in 1923.

Panjandrum pandemonium

One of the best jobs in the Second World War must have been working for the British Directorate of Miscellaneous Weapons Development (DMWD). This was essentially a group of ex-public school* boys in uniform tasked with devising devious new weapons. By 1943 Allied plans were already afoot for the eventual invasion and liberation of Nazi-held Europe. The Wheezers and Dodgers (as the DMWD were nicknamed) were asked to come up with something that could create a gap through the coastal defences of Hitler's Atlantic Wall, allowing attacking troops and tanks to clear the killing zone of the landing beaches quickly.

What they came up with was named the panjandrum, and this was not the only bizarre thing about it. It essentially consisted of a large wooden barrel (about 6 feet long and 3 feet in diameter), packed with the best part of two tons of high explosive, forming the axle that joined two wooden wheels, each 10 feet in diameter and 1 foot thick. Around the circumference of each wheel were placed a number of 20-pound cordite rockets, angled in such a way that, when ignited, they would set the whole thing rolling at a planned speed of upto 60mph. It was to be launched from the bow ramp of a landing craft pointed at the target stretch of defences, so it would race straight up the beach, its weight and speed giving it the momentum to flatten barbed wire entanglements, then smash into its target where it would be detonated.

Having built the prototype of this potential war-winner in a top-secret facility in Devon, the development team (including the author Nevil Shute) took it for its first test run on 7 September 1943 at Westward Ho! beach – a popular holiday spot. Of course no high explosives were on board, that would have been silly, the equivalent weight being provided by sand ballast. Even so the astonished

* For non-British readers, the 'public' in 'public schools' means 'private', and there you can get a truly comprehensive education; publicly funded schools are called 'comprehensive schools' and there you generally don't. Simple.

bathers were treated to the sight of what was effectively a giant Catherine wheel hurtling up the beach. It travelled straight and true for about 50 yards before some of the rockets on the right wheel went out prematurely, causing it to veer off to the left before toppling over. Back to the drawing board.

Back at the top-secret facility the boffins decided that what this unpredictable monster needed was lots more rockets. They also tried attaching a third wheel for stability and took it back to the beach, where their top-secret test was again watched by crowds of onlookers. This time the panjandrum had barely fizzed and whirled its way out of the shallows when rockets started breaking loose, firing off over the heads of the spectators before exploding. Fortunately, the contraption then performed a u-turn and headed back out to sea. On subsequent tests, the third wheel was dropped in favour of steel cables attached to either side like reins so that it could be steered from the landing craft, and of course more rockets, seventy altogether. The beast refused to be leashed in this way and snapped the steel cables, which whipped around as it swerved off course, adding a new danger to that of the now familiar one of loose rockets shooting off hither and thither.

The final test was conducted in January 1944 in front of assembled top brass and an official photographer to film proceedings. True to form, the panjandrum roared through the surf and up the sand before veering off course and chasing the terrified photographer along the beach while the startled admirals and generals were sent diving for cover by the rockets it jettisoned with mischievous abandon. Now that senior officers as well as the general public had been endangered, the project was swiftly cancelled.

What the Habakkuk?

By 1941 the imminent threat of a German invasion of Britain had passed but the relentless attacks of U-boat 'wolfpacks' on vital shipping in the Atlantic threatened to strangle Britain's war effort and starve her into submission. Aircraft were the most effective weapons against submarines but vast stretches of the Atlantic sea lanes were beyond the range of shore-based planes. Britain had too few aircraft carriers and the aircraft those carried were too few and too small to project sufficient air power over the necessary area (a lesson well learnt eh? At least they had *some* aircraft on them!). Besides, aircraft carriers themselves were vulnerable to air attack unless protected by more ships. What was needed was a giant unsinkable aircraft carrier. 'An unsinkable ship? Impossible', I hear you say 'They said the *Titanic* was unsinkable and look what happened to her'. And you make a good point of course, but what if you don't look at the *Titanic* but at the iceberg that sank her? Icebergs are unsinkable so why not take an iceberg, stick some engines and a runway on it and hey presto! You have an airfield that you can put in the middle of the ocean and those pesky Jerries won't be able to do a thing about it. This, in essence, was the thinking of British inventor Geoffrey Pyke. He proposed the idea, with some refinement, to Lord Mountbatten at the Admiralty and he in turn recommended it to Churchill as worth a try.

The project was codenamed Habakkuk, a reference to one of the less well-known books of the *Old Testament*. The prophet Habakkuk asked God why he was not doing enough smiting of sinners and was told 'be utterly amazed, for I am going to do something in your days that you would not believe, even if you were told'; so it's quite an appropriate codename for what was intended to be the last word in oceanic smiting of baddies.

The plan, it must be clarified, was not to convert an existing iceberg, that would just be silly. No, the far more sensible scheme adopted was to build their own out of blocks of ice and then put upon it all the necessary hangars, workshops and accommodation required by a normal aircraft carrier. Initially the idea was to have it towed around by conventional ships but it didn't take long to decide to stick a couple of diesel engines and screw propellers on it. The Royal Navy also decided they might as well make the runways long enough to take the heaviest bombers for extra effective smiting. This was sheer genius, an unsinkable vessel made from water, the cheapest and most abundant material on the planet.

Of course it didn't take long before someone pointed out that ice melts, which might make it less than useful as far south as the mid-Atlantic where more air coverage was really needed. Pyke offered an answer to this in the form of Pykrete, a frozen mixture of water and wood pulp that could be easily cast in any shape required.

Pykrete was still unsinkable but structurally stronger than pure ice and it melted more slowly.

The design that eventually crystallized on the drawing board was to be constructed of 280,000 Pykrete blocks and would be a monstrous 2,000 feet long, 300 feet wide and 200 feet deep, with an astounding displacement of around 2,000,000 tons. The hull was to be made 40 feet thick, rendering it torpedo proof. To put all this in perspective, the largest warship afloat today is the nuclear-powered aircraft carrier USS *Enterprise*, which is 1,123 feet long and has a comparatively puny displacement of 94,781 tons. Okay, so the ice ship's projected top speed was only 7 knots, but that was still 7 knots faster than most island bases.

Progress with turning this into reality was a bit slow. Tests to determine the optimum composition for Pykrete were carried out in a secret high-tech laboratory (well, it was behind the carcasses hanging in a requisitioned meat locker in Smithfield Market). In case you are thinking of making your own super ice ship the winning formula was 86 per cent water and 14 per cent wood pulp. However, a problem was also discovered: although Pykrete resisted actual melting in water, it exhibited 'plastic flow', meaning it would stretch and distort so the large vessel would gradually sag in the middle unless kept fully frozen at −16°. So the design was amended to accommodate refrigerating machinery and reinforcing steel girders.

By 1943 the Admiralty was ready to order a prototype built on Lake Patricia in Canada. Built with the labour of conscientious objectors who were never told about the intended smiting, this test model was scaled down sómewhat. It measured just 60 feet by 30 feet and displaced a mere 1,000 tons, but tested the basics of Pykrete construction with embedded refrigeration ducting (even once the tests were finished it took a couple of years to melt fully). Churchill was sufficiently impressed to order the first full-sized ship to be started as soon as possible and it was hoped to have it ready by 1944.

Unfortunately, as technical difficulties continued to slow progress, the project was gradually sidelined and in the end abandoned altogether. In part this was because it was gradually realized that while the water for the ice was freely available, the materials for the refrigeration plants, miles of ducting and thousands of tons of steel reinforcement were scarce and perhaps better used elsewhere. This was especially the case since someone had now thought to ask the Portuguese dictator, Antonio de Oliveira Salazar, if the Allies could rent a patch of the Azores islands to fly their aircraft from since these were already handily placed in the Atlantic, at least as unsinkable as any ice ship and not nearly so chilly to live on. Salazar, despite previously being quite cosy with the Nazis, took the cash and the Allies moved in during Operation Alacrity in October 1943.

Hitler's pets

As the tide of the Second World War turned and Hitler's 'thousand-year Reich' looked like falling short by 990 years or so, his self esteem must have taken quite a knock. And those amusing songs about him only having one testicle cannot have helped much either. The well known principle that men drive big cars to compensate for inadequacies in other areas (I drive a Nissan Micra since you ask) probably accounts for the little corporal's obsession with ever-larger super weapons.

At a time when the Allies were liberating Europe with swarms of tanks that tipped the scales at a modest 30 tons or so, the Germans had developed the monstrous PzKpfw VI Tiger II Königstiger (or King Tiger), which weighed in at just under 67 tonnes. Its 88mm main gun could easily destroy any Allied tank in service, while armour up to 6 inches (150mm) thick meant it could shrug off most return fire. The King Tiger was the heaviest and most powerful tank to actually see service in the Second World War. Hitler's ego, however, still wanted something bigger.

The project to build a super-heavy tank was actually ordered in 1942 from Porsche, not the last mid-life crisis they've profited from. The result was the ironically named Maus (Mouse) which weighed in at a whopping 188 tonnes. The Maus' main armament was to be a 128mm gun. Where most tanks carried a machine gun as secondary armament, the Maus had a 75mm gun (the main armament on most Allied tanks such as the Sherman) and a machine gun for good measure. The Maus was thick-skinned too with armour almost 8 inches (200mm) thick.

Fortunately for the Allies, the Germans had overlooked a couple of minor details. Firstly, they didn't have a tank engine powerful enough to propel this beast at more than a slug-like 12mph and then unreliably. Secondly, it was soon realized that the Maus was too big and heavy for existing road bridges, so wouldn't be able to cross any of the many European rivers that were too deep to wade. Even if a tank's hull is watertight, combustion engines need to be able to 'breathe'. This can be achieved with snorkels but the Porsche designers spent a lot of time developing a more elaborate solution which would allow deeper rivers to be crossed. The mice would work in pairs, one driving fully submerged across the river bed, powered by electricity passed via a cable from its partner on the river bank, which would be using its petrol engine as a generator. Such were the developmental problems that Porsche were still tinkering with the only two prototypes when Germany was over-run by the relatively puny allied tanks. One now graces a Soviet museum.

Even the Maus, impractically large as it was, did not touch the sides of Hitler's megalomaniacal hunger for a really big tank. The Maus would have been dwarfed by the planned P.1000 Land-kreuzer, almost inevitably codenamed Ratte (Rat). The design approved by Hitler was the brainchild of Wilhelm Grote, one of the directors of Krupp. Grote's usual role was designing submarines and it showed in the Ratte. The beast was to weigh 1,000 tonnes and measure almost 115 feet (35 metres) long, 46 feet (14 metres) wide and stand 36 feet (11 metres) high. The great weight would be carried on six sets of tracks.

Like the Maus, the Ratte would carry a 128mm gun, but for the Ratte this was only a close-protection back-up. For the main arma-ment Grote would simply modify the turret of a Gneisenau-class battleship with twin 280mm (11-inch) guns capable of lobbing a 700-pound shell about 25 miles. The Ratte, which would make a tempting target for air attack, would also pack a battery of eight 20mm anti-aircraft guns and a few machine guns for last-ditch self defence if anything ever ventured close enough. Armour up to 9 inches thick would allow the Ratte to laugh off return fire from any enemy tank and all but the heaviest artillery. Within its protective shell, the crew of twenty or so would be well catered for with bunks, an infirmary, flushing toilets and even a garage for a couple of BMW motorcycles.

Grote would also draw on his maritime background for the propulsion system, proposing to use either two submarine engines or eight of the sort used by 'E-boat' fast attack craft. Either combination would generate in excess of 16,000hp, power equivalent to about twenty-two Tiger IIs or a dozen or so modern Challenger tanks. This was apparently expected to allow a top speed of 28mph, though this seems optimistic. The Rat's engines would be fitted with the same snorkels that allowed U-boats to run on diesel without surfacing, but in any case its great height would allow it to simply wade across most rivers without difficulty. Perhaps fortunately for the Allies, the project, though approved, never got beyond the drawing board.

Incredibly, Krupp proposed and Hitler approved, an even larger vehicle. The appropriately named P.1500 Monster was to weigh 1,500 tonnes. Technically a self-propelled artillery piece rather than a true tank, this was intended to carry a single 800mm gun that could lob a 7-tonne shell up to 29 miles (47km). Perhaps fortunately for the Allies, both Ratte and Monster were cancelled by Albert Speer, Germany's Minister of Armaments and War Production, before they even got off the drawing board.

Dog-gone disaster

While the military use of dogs is commonplace (we are all used to the idea of dogs being used to sniff out explosives, track down fugitives or to guard facilities), one variation on the theme is generally deplored not only for its cynical betrayal of the human-canine bond but for the ineptness of its execution. The Soviets, while very forward thinking in developing their own modern tank forces, also tried some decidedly low-tech, half-baked methods to defeat the panzers of the invading Germans. The famous anti-tank dog, however, was not the product of desperation caused by the early successes of the German blitzkrieg – the Russians had been training dogs for this role for at least a decade.

The idea was a simple one: train dogs to run under enemy tanks carrying explosives that could be detonated against its thinly-armoured underside. Initially the idea was apparently for the dogs to drop off the explosives, releasing the carrying harness with their teeth, and escape to a safe distance before a timed fuse triggered the explosion. Unfortunately the dogs proved unable to undo the buckle and in any case a delayed explosion gave the target tank a chance to move off. So the process was simplified. The explosives on the dogs' backs would instead be fitted with a vertical wooden lever which would cause instant detonation when knocked flat by the action of the dog crawling under the tank. The dog of course would be blown to bits too.

These poor pooches were first unleashed in anger during the desperate defensive battles of 1941 and 1942. There were some successes but generally the tactic ran into some unforeseen hitches. Chief among these were that the dogs had been trained by placing their food under Russian tanks. It was probably the familiar smell of Soviet diesel (German tanks had petrol engines), that caused some of the hungry dogs to run for the nearest Russian tanks. Others were simply too scared of the advancing enemy and the general cacophony of the battlefield and ran back to leap into the trenches with their horrified handlers, with disastrous results.

The Germans responded by issuing orders for all and any non-German dogs to be shot on sight. The Russians used the tactic less and less as the war went on but training of anti-tank dogs by the Soviet army continued until June 1996.[72]

Perhaps inspired by their Soviet allies, the US army flirted with the idea of making similar use of dogs, but to destroy bunkers and buildings. The dogs, again carrying explosives on their backs, were to be trained to run into the target structure and sit down until a timer triggered the explosion. In training at Fort Belvoir, however, the dogs frequently ran back out to their handlers and the project was cancelled in December 1943. The Americans also devoted considerable resources, including the purchase of an island in the Mississippi River, to the idea of using waves of attack dogs, released from landing craft, to lead the invasion of Japanese-held Pacific islands. Japanese-Americans were induced to volunteer as authentic training targets but the dogs did not respond well to the training, which included live shellfire, and the idea was abandoned.

The flying tank

The Second World War saw the use of paratroopers by both Axis and Allied armies. Air-dropping was a great way to get troops behind enemy lines to seize vital objectives such as bridges and airfields in surprise attacks. One major problem, however, was how to provide lightly-armed paratroopers with sufficient firepower to see off enemy tanks and other forces until the land-based reinforcements could reach them. The Western Allies and Germany approached this challenge by developing large gliders and small tanks to fit into them. The gliders could land in any reasonably flat field, delivering much-needed support to the troops.

The Soviets, typically, took a different approach. First they tried strapping light tanks to the bellies of bombers which would simply fly and land with them, but this required a suitable airfield to be available. Then they tried dropping them by parachute or just into water, which usually resulted in the loss of the vehicle and in any case required the crew to be dropped separately, leaving both crew and vehicle vulnerable for some time. In the occupation of Bessarabia in 1940 they successfully dropped some tanks from beneath heavy bombers flying at very low altitude, but this would be too risky for these aircraft in a defended area where they might come under heavy fire. Finally they opted for a tank that itself became a glider by means of strap-on wings and tail. The A-40 Tanka Krylla (Tank Wings) was designed by aircraft designer Oleg Antonov to be fitted to a T-60 light tank. It would be towed within gliding distance of the target area by a bomber and released. When it had landed the crew could jump out, quickly detach the wings and tail and be ready for action.

The first test was carried out on 2 September 1942 using a Tupolev TB-3 bomber as the towing aircraft. Unfortunately the glider/tank caused so much drag that the TB-3 had to cut it adrift shortly after takeoff to avoid crashing. The tank itself, however, glided down nicely, just as intended, and its pilot/driver was able to shed his wings and drive back to the airfield. A little prematurely, perhaps, the project was abandoned. The Soviets went back to experimenting with air-dropping vehicles on parachutes and had perfected it sufficiently by the mid-1970s to safely drop light armoured fighting vehicles like the 5.5-ton BRDM-1 scout car, complete with crew.

Ilya Muromets Bomber

The S-22 Ilya Muromets, the world's first four-engined bomber, was the military version of the S-22 Russky Vityaz, a passenger plane which first took to the skies in May 1913. Bear in mind that this was less than a decade after Orville Wright made the first powered flight laying spread-eagled on the fragile, kite-like *Flyer*, and you will see it was an immense leap forward in technology. Built by the Russian Baltic Railway Coach Works, it looked like someone had just strapped large wings and engines to a railway carriage, and it had much of the luxury. It boasted a spacious, heated cabin capable of carrying sixteen passengers in comfy chairs, electric lighting provided by a wind-powered generator, a washroom with toilet and a bedroom. Where the Wright brothers had managed a hop of 120 feet (which would barely have cleared the S-22's wingspan of 100 feet), the Ilya Muromets could stay aloft for five hours while carrying a 660lb payload (or twice that if just carrying fuel).

Despite these remarkably advanced features, its designer apparently had little faith in its reliability since the design also incorporated a cupboard full of spare parts and doors on either side of the cockpit that allowed the crew to walk out along the lower wings for in-flight engine maintenance! This caution is perhaps understandable given that aero engines were still in their infancy but also given particular previous experiences of the aircraft's designer and test-pilot, Igor Sikorsky. In 1911, aged just 22 years old, Sikorsky obtained his pilot's licence flying an aircraft he had designed and built himself. However, later that same year he wrecked this aircraft when a mosquito in the petrol caused a blockage that stalled the engine. In June 1913, the prototype of the S-22 was destroyed on the ground by the engine falling off another aircraft (a single-engined plane at that – oops!) as it came in to land.

Despite the designer's concerns over the engines (which were also encased in 5mm steel armour), the Ilya Muromets proved very successful on wartime duty with the Imperial Russian Air Service, though there were never enough of them to make a real strategic impact. In addition to an 800lb bomb load each aircraft bristled with up to nine defensive machine guns, including one manned by a very brave chap at the extremity of the tail, completely cut off from the rest of the crew. The enemy only ever succeeded in shooting down one of them and this only after the Ilya Muromets had shot down three of its four attackers.

Mother's little helpers

The Ilya Muromets aside, heavy bombers flying over enemy territory were generally vulnerable to defending enemy fighter planes. Fighters had the speed and agility to catch them, outmanoeuvre them and shoot them down. The best way to counter a fighter is with another fighter, but these generally could not carry sufficient fuel to accompany heavy bombers all the way to their targets on long-range strategic bombing missions. To overcome this problem, several nations experimented with the 'mother ship' idea in which a long-range aircraft would carry its own fighter escort fixed to it and launch them when needed.

The idea originated in the First World War with the British who tried launching Sopwith Camel fighters from airships. For a short period in the 1920s the US Army Air Force had an operational unit of Curtiss Sparrowhawk fighters flying from airships. But the Soviets were definitely the most successful in this field. In the 1930s they experimented with a Tupolev TB-1 or TB-3 heavy bomber carrying up to eight fighters attached above and/or below the wings and piggy-back style on the fuselage. The smaller planes ran their engines during flight, which provided the necessary power for the whole combination to get in the air and stay there, but could draw fuel from the mother ship. The original idea was for the smaller planes to be able to be both launched and re-attached in flight but, although testing proved it was possible, docking proved too risky for operational use. Instead the fighters would feed off the mother ship on the outward journey, be released near the target area with their own fuel supply intact and fly the return leg independently.

The configuration finally settled upon consisted of a TB-3 bomber carrying a Polikarpov I-16 fighter under each wing. These were used with some success in the early stages of the Second World War. On these missions, the I-16s were actually used as fighter-bombers to make low-level attacks against pinpoint targets that the heavy bombers would have been unable to hit (bombing from high altitude, the only level at which heavy bombers were reasonably safe from air defences, was still very inaccurate in those days). The TB-3 acted only as a ferry to get her babies closer to the target with a heavier payload of bombs than they could otherwise have carried (each carried two 500lb bombs) and sufficient fuel for the return trip. Once released, the vulnerable mother ship could simply turn back for home without having to enter the enemy's air defences. In this manner, several successful attacks were made on Romanian oil fields and vital bridges.

During the Second World War the British solved the problem of protecting long-range bombers by flying at night (the only draw-back being that they couldn't hit anything smaller than a city and not always those), while the Americans flew by day protected by fighters carrying their own extra fuel in disposable drop tanks. In the post-war period, however, the development of massive jet bombers capable of the much longer missions needed to reach potential Soviet targets, led the US Air force to renewed experimen-tation with 'parasite' aircraft. The XF-35 Goblin was being purpose-built to be carried in the internal bomb bay of the huge B-36 bomber. It was intended that a proportion of each B-36 formation would be converted to mother ships, each giving birth to four or five Goblins during the dangerous final stages of long range missions to protect the bombers from enemy fighters. However, there were problems. The Goblin could only fly for thirty minutes and so would have to return to the belly of the B-36 if it was to get home and this proved dangerous to both aircraft during trials; furthermore the baby Goblin, a comical little aircraft that looked like an egg with stubby wings bolted on, would have been no match for the defensive fighters it might encounter. Only two prototypes were made. There were later experiments with proven fighters attaching in-flight to the wingtips of bombers but these too were abandoned, largely due to the development of in-flight refuelling of escort fighters as a viable alternative.

Nazi rocket planes

In the later stages of the Second World War, the Germans desper-ately needed an answer to the swarms of Allied heavy bombers blasting the bejabbers out of their Fatherland day and night. But rather than concentrating all their diminishing resources on producing more fighter aircraft based on their existing, successful designs, much effort was expended in the search for novel wonder weapons. Several designers were convinced salvation lay with rocket powered interceptors.

Rockets must not be confused with the more sophisticated jet, which was being developed simultaneously. A rocket simply ignites fuel in a combustion chamber and the resultant explosive expansion of gases, directed out of the exhaust, propels the plane in the opposite direction. Rocket planes were effectively large fireworks with tail, wings and a pilot added. Their great advantage was incredible acceleration and rate of climb, allowing them to take off and quickly reach high-flying bomber formations as they passed overhead. The only type to enter service before the war ended, the Messerschmitt Me163 Komet, managed almost 700 mph in tests but could easily do 550mph in level flight (Allied escort fighters could reach around 450mph) and it could climb to 39,000 feet in just three minutes. The design of the aircraft itself, developed from a glider, had excellent handling characteristics, would not stall or spin and yet was very manoeuvrable.

So much for the plus side. On the negative side, rockets are very inefficient in their fuel consumption, giving the aircraft very short endurance. The Komet could only fly for seven and a half minutes before having to glide back down to land, during which time it was vulnerable to enemy fighters. While the rocket was still burning, the plane was actually too fast for effective use of its armament which consisted of two 30mm cannon. These had a powerful punch but were only accurate at short range so the pilot had only a brief moment to line up and fire a couple of shots before he zoomed past the much-slower moving bomber and had to be very lucky to score a hit.

The pilots usually managed one quick burst as they roared up through the bomber formation and one more as they dived back through it and that was their lot.

An ingenious attempt was made to resolve this. The forward-firing armament was replaced by ten 50mm cannon mounted in the wings to fire upwards and linked to a light-sensitive cell. When the Komet flew under the enemy bomber, the cell would be in its shadow and the cannon would be automatically triggered to fire. It was apparently tried in action and a bomber was destroyed in this way but these guns could only fire once.

Then came the tricky task of landing, which was always a bit hairy since the Komet, to save the drag and weight of complex landing gear, jettisoned its undercarriage shortly after take-off. For landing it bumped down on its reinforced, keel-like fuselage. And these were the problems experienced when everything went to plan. The two-part fuel used was so unstable that the aircraft sometimes simply exploded in flight or even while still sitting on the airfield and it was so toxic and corrosive that the pilots had to fly in the discomfort of special protective suits. Far from being the wonder-weapon Hitler hoped for, Komets destroyed just sixteen Allied aircraft while they suffered fifteen aircraft lost in return, five destroyed by enemy aircraft and the rest by various accidents.

Even so, the Me-163 was a successful design compared to the Bachem Ba-349 Natter (Viper). This offered all the same shortfalls of highly unstable fuel and short flight time but lacked the Komet's manoeuvrability. The Natter did not require a runway, instead blasting off vertically from a pylon like the later space rockets. It used the same rocket motor as the Komet plus two extra rocket boosters fitted externally and jettisoned shortly after takeoff.

No sophisticated manoeuvres were expected, certainly nothing as tricky as landing, which was just as well since the only pilots who could be found for the project were fanatical but inexperienced teenagers from the Hitler Youth. When the pilot had recovered sufficiently from the incredible forces exerted by being hurtled skyward, high above the enemy bombers and already out of fuel, he would point his aircraft down at one of them. An early plan was considered to give the Viper a solid concrete nose cone with which to ram the enemy plane but the Germans rejected this in favour of a battery of unguided rockets. The young pilot would dive on a bomber, fire off the salvo of up to twenty-four rockets all at once and then bail out.

Bailing out was to be achieved by undoing his safety harness, detaching the expendable nose section and deploying a large parachute attached to the rear of the aircraft. The rapid slowing of the tail section would whip the pilot's seat from under him and he would fall out of the now-open front where the nose cone used to be. The pilot and tail section would then descend safely on their separate parachutes, ready for another mission. At least that was the plan. Only two vertical test launches were made. The first, using a dummy pilot, went well in that the dummy pilot landed safely but the tail section made a heavy landing and the engine exploded on the airfield. On the second attempt the faulty canopy was torn off in the climb, carrying away the headrest of the pilot (a real live one this time) and breaking his neck. The project was abandoned.

The Germans supplied rocket technology to their Japanese allies. Their attempt to copy the Me-163 interceptor failed when one of the submarines carrying the components of a prototype was lost en route. They did, however, produce hundreds of the rocket-powered Yokosuka M-11. This was purpose built for suicide (*kamikaze* – literally 'divine wind') missions and was really a piloted anti-ship missile, rather than a true aeroplane. Packed with high explosives and rocket fuel, it was carried and then dropped from another aircraft, whereupon the pilot would set it on course for an Allied warship, fire up its rockets and guide it in to impact. Nearly 700 were built and these accounted for the sinking of three ships and the damaging of a few more. The Japanese gave it the poetic code-name Ohka (Cherry Blossom), while the Americans knew it by the codename Baka (Idiot).

To the bat cave!

Definitely the battiest weapon developed in the Second World War was the American Project X-Ray. This was a weapon designed to inflict terror and suffering on millions of defenceless people, so it is perhaps not surprising that it was thought up by a dentist, Dr Lytle Adams. It had its genesis on the very 'day of infamy' that Japan attacked Pearl Harbor, signalling war with the United States. When he heard the news on the radio, Adams was just returning from a holiday in New Mexico where he had been fascinated by the spectacle of millions of bats returning to their caves to roost. Inspired by a desire for revenge, he came up with the fiendish idea of dropping millions of live bats over Japan, each carrying a tiny incendiary device on a timer to set whole cities ablaze. After a bit more thought he sent his proposal to the White House in early 1942 and it was approved by President Roosevelt. The fact that Adams was a friend of Eleanor Roosevelt probably accounts for it not going straight in the presidential bin. The President took good care to write 'This man is *not* a nut' across the proposal before he forwarded it to the military for development.

The details of the weapon worked out at Carlsbad Army Air Force Base in New Mexico were quite ingenious. The bats used were Mexican free-tailed bats, each weighing only half an ounce (14 grams) but capable of carrying twice its own bodyweight. They were easily rendered docile and manageable by cooling them, allowing each to have a purpose-built timed incendiary device weighing less than an ounce clipped to their chest. The armed bats were then carefully packed into specially designed bombs, each containing 1,040 individual compartments arranged in a concertina-like stack of twenty-six connected trays. The bombs would be dropped from high altitude in daylight and at 1,000 feet a parachute would deploy to slow its descent, the outer casing would drop away and the inner concertina of trays would open up. The bats, now warming up, would wake up to find themselves falling through the air in broad daylight and fly off across a wide area to roost in the nearest dark nook or cranny they could find, hopefully under the eaves of Japanese houses, which of course were mainly made of wood and paper. Sometime later, all the incendiary devices would go off simultaneously, overwhelming the local fire-fighting services.

Development was not without its hitches, such as when some armed bats escaped, roosted under a fuel storage tank and burned down part of the Carlsbad facility. But at least this proved the concept had wings and by December 1943 all was ready for the first full test at Dugway Proving Ground in Utah, where a replica Japanese village had been erected. It all went perfectly and the village was quickly and completely destroyed. Yes, perhaps the most surprising thing about this crazy idea is that it actually worked. The only reason it was never used is that it was going to take until mid-1945 before enough bats and bombs could be produced for a bombing campaign on a scale likely to force the Japanese into surrender. The atomic bomb appeared to be further ahead in development. The cancellation of Project X-Ray saved the lives of millions of innocent bats, but who can say what would have happened if this non-radioactive alternative had been pursued instead?

Chapter 17

Towards the Future – Robot Wars

It seems fitting to end with a look to the future of warfare. Modern technology is moving so fast that things that previously seemed like science fiction are actually being developed. For example, 'cloaking' devices to effectively make objects invisible to the human eye have been proved theoretically possible, even if it currently takes a huge apparatus to hide something so small that it was barely visible anyway. Similarly lasers for use on ships and aircraft are looking increasingly viable. But in one particular area of research a much more immediate revolution is getting under way and that is in the development of robots.

Unmanned aircraft, or 'drones', have been in use since the Vietnam War but are now increasingly commonplace with a thriving market for rapidly-improving products from various manufacturers. Initially these were developed as unarmed reconnaissance platforms but they are increasingly used to strike targets with guided missiles and are thought to have accounted for a significant proportion of Al-Qaeda's leadership. On land, too, unmanned vehicles have been used for years, largely for bomb disposal. Currently these are remotely controlled by a human operator rather than autonomous true robots. This makes great use of the agile thumb skills of modern soldiers of the Xbox generation since the remote control systems utilize games console handsets with little or no modification. This is about to change, however, since numerous companies are actively working on various kinds of true robots with greater levels of autonomy.

Here are just a few of my favourite military robots coming soon(ish) to a battlefield near you.

Battlefield Extraction-Assist Robot (BEAR)

As its name suggests, BEAR is a robot designed to assist in extracting casualties from dangerous situations. Until now, if a soldier is injured in an exposed position, perhaps in an area where mines, IEDs or snipers are still suspected, his commander and comrades faced a difficult dilemma. They can't just leave the poor guy (or gal) lying there bleeding but sending more soldiers in to get them might just result in further casualties. Now they can instead call for a BEAR. Above the waist, BEAR is vaguely the shape of a real bear, with torso, head and two arms ending in elongated hands. Below the waist is a tracked chassis like a little tank. The arms, with their long curved fingers are capable of scooping up and carrying up to 500 pounds (227kg) or can alternatively drag the wounded soldier by his webbing. Of course a soldier laying in the dust, battered and bleeding, scared and perhaps concussed by an IED blast, might find it a little traumatic to be approached and picked up in the claw-like hands of a machine. But the designers, Vecna Technologies, have thought of that and put a cute little bear face, with big eyes and little ears on it. 'We thought it might give the casualty something to smile about' said a spokesman.

BigDog

For the foreseeable future, technology will not completely replace 'boots on the ground', that is boots with real flesh and blood men in them. The lessons of the campaigns in Iraq and Afghanistan have prompted the rapid development and introduction of a wide range of clever gadgets to help the modern infantryman do his job safely and efficiently: everything from folding ladders to miniature remote-controlled reconnaissance aircraft and, of course, the return of body armour after an absence of about 400 years. These things are all useful but the PBI (Poor Bloody Infantry) has to carry a heavier load than ever. So the US military has been looking at ways to ease this burden, leaving them fresher for the fight. One solution that is being considered is BigDog, under development by Boston Dynamics.

As the Boston Dynamics website points out, less than half of the world's landmass is accessible to existing wheeled or tracked vehicles, whereas legged animals can go more or less anywhere. BigDog is a four-legged robot that replicates the complex walking, running, even jumping motions of a living quadruped. It has been tested on ice and steep slopes. The demonstration video even shows the 'handler' trying to kick it over from the side but it skitters sideways just like a real dog would, then corrects itself and carries on. It is really quite eerie.

Despite the name, what all the research and expense has achieved is basically to reinvent the pack mule. BigDog's primary purpose (for now) is just to carry the soldier's kit on its back. It can be instructed to follow a particular soldier, recognizing him or her by a transmitter worn on their back. It will tag along dutifully at a set distance but not blindly – an array of sensors makes it aware of the terrain to be traversed so it can pick its way through safely.

BigDog is not yet ready for action, not so far as I can see from the developer's website anyway. There are at least a couple of problems to be ironed out. The first is that it would, in its current state, make it impossible to sneak up on any enemy. Powered as it is by a 15hp go-kart engine it emits a continuous loud buzz. Secondly, although BigDog set the world record for the longest non-stop journey without refuelling by a quadrupedal robot, this was still just under 13 miles.

Vegetarian robot tank

The US military are already testing unmanned ground combat vehicles with sufficient autonomy that they can be given a mission and be left to get on with it, without the guidance of a button-pushing operative. Sensing the terrain around them they can decide on the best route from A to B, recalculating if necessary as the situation changes and carry out a mission, such as reconnaissance or attacking or guarding a specified location. They could theoretically be used to identify and attack enemy troops though the official line on this at the moment is that the decision to use lethal force will always referred back to a human commander.

Such vehicles, while capable of autonomous decision making within certain parameters, will still be limited by dependence on fuel supply. However, ways are already being sought to get round this limitation to create a combat vehicle that can be left out on patrol, reconnaissance or sentry duty for very extended periods, if not indefinitely, independent of fuel depots. The concept, put forward by Robotic Technology Inc (RTI) in 2003, and sponsored by the Defence Advanced Research Projects Agency, is for a tank that runs on bio-fuel gathered and processed in the field. Early press speculation about the project sparked sufficient concern about a flesh-eating robot for RTI to issue a statement on their website asserting that the tank was strictly vegetarian. Rumours that it might be intended to feed on enemy dead was rebutted by a reminder that 'Desecration of the dead is a war crime under Article 15 of the Geneva Conventions, and is certainly not something sanctioned by DARPA, Cyclone [who make the bio-fuel engine] or RTI.'

The Energetically Autonomous Tactical Robot (EATR) will use a robotic harvesting arm, or a mower arrangement where appropriate, to feed trees, shrubs and other vegetation into its hopper, where it will be used as bio-fuel. Not a fussy eater, it will be able to supplement this with whatever other fuels are available, such as domestic refuse, coal or cooking oil, as well as conventional petrol or diesel and even solar power. The resultant freedom from supply bases has obvious military advantages. Although EATRs could ultimately act alone for some missions, their first use is likely to be in support of conventional forces, for which they can act as a mobile generator to recharge the batteries of their radios and various other gadgets. When the other troops rest, it could pop off for a nibble of the nearest tree.

EATR would be quite a hungry beast. It is expected to be able to gather and eat 150lbs (68kg) of wood or vegetation in fifteen minutes. If this was wood, the most efficient, this would produce energy equivalent to a gallon of gasoline. But EATR would require 500lbs (227kg) of lush green vegetation to achieve the same effect. How much it could do with this energy depends on the type of vehicle the EATR concept is applied to, which is not yet known. But a Hummer, the ubiquitous utility and patrol vehicle of the US Army, only manages about 12 miles to the gallon. So, even if enough food is available in the area of operations, EATR is going to have to spend quite a lot of time grazing rather than actually conducting its primary mission. And what happens if the prospective enemies of the future happen to be in arid areas with scarce vegetation, which has to be a distinct possibility? And, as a final thought, even if EATR is deployed in lush areas, has anyone considered the effect on the 'hearts and minds' of the local populace when they find a herd of hungry robot tanks munching through their crop fields or scavenging among their trash cans?

Notes

Chapter 1: War Elephants and How to Beat Them

1. John M. Kistler, *War Elephants* (Lincoln and London, 2007) pp. 2 and 8. Elephants were certainly being used in war by 1500 BC in Syria, though they may well have already been in use in Chinese and Indian armies for some time by then.
2. Muhammed Nazim, *The Life and Times of Sultan Mahmud of Ghazna* (New Delhi, 1971), quoted in Kistler, *War Elephants*, pp. 191–2.
3. *The Baltimore Sun*, 31 July 1995, available at http://articles.baltimoresun.com/1995-07-31/features/1995212131_1_gantt-sawmill-elephants
4. Anonymous, The African Wars, 84, published with Julius Caesar, *The Civil War*, edited and translated by John Carter (Oxford, 1998).
5. Kistler, *War Elephants*, p. 280 citing John Ranking, *Historical Researches on the Wars and Sports of the Mongols and Romans: In Which Elephants and Wild Beasts Were Employed or Slain* (London, 1826), p. 280.
6. My thanks to James Opie for sending me the photo of the Britons stilt walker.
7. Nicholas Hobbes, *Essential Militaria* (London, 2003).
8. Kistler, *War Elephants*, p. 213, citing Abu'l-Fazl, *The Akbarnama of Abu'l-Fazl: A History of the Reign of Akbar*, vol. 3, translated by H. Beveridge (Calcutta, 1939).

Chapter 2: Ignominious Deaths

9. Roy Ingleton, *Kent VCs* (Barnsley, 2010), pp. 10–14
10. Thanks to Timothy Venning for this one. Roger of Wendover and Henry of Huntingdon are the key medieval sources for this, both of which, it should be noted, are much later than the events they describe.
11. Chris Bishop, *Kreigsmarine U-Boats 1939–45* (Spellmount, Staplehurst, 2006), p. 14.

Chapter 4: A Misplaced Sense of Honour

12. C.J. Peers, *Ancient Chinese Armies 1500–200 BC* (London, 1990), pp. 13–14.
13. Philip Matyszak, *Chronicle of the Roman Republic* (London, 2003), pp. 78–9.
14. Mike Loades, *Swords and Swordsmen* (Barnsley, 2009), p. 239.
15. Cited by Donald Norman Moran in his well-researched article 'Major Patrick Ferguson: The Sharp Shooter Who Almost Won the War for the British', available at www.american revolution.org

Notes

Chapter 5: Suicide Mission

16. Mike Loades, *Swords and Swordsmen* (Barnsley, 2009), p. 239.
17. Chris Peers, *Ancient Chinese Armies*, (Oxford), p. 15.
18. All the quotes in this passage are from Josephus, *The Jewish War*, translated by G.A. Williamson, with notes and appendices by E. Mary Smallwood (London, 1981), Book III; see Appendix F for notes on the alternative version.

Chapter 6: Soldiers' Accessories

19. Geoffrey Regan, *The Guinness Book of Military Blunders* (London, 1991), p. 124 (American Civil War) and p. 181 (Indian troops).
20. Philip Matyszak, *The Classical Compendium* (London, 2009), p. 93.
21. Michael J. Winey, 'Clothes Encounters of Three Kinds' in *Vignettes of Military History*, No. 93 (20 March 1978, US Army Military History Institute), p. 43, kindly sent to me by Peter G. Tsouras.

Chapter 7: The Gods are With Us

22. Herodotus, *The Histories*, I.46–80,
23. Herodotus, *The Histories*, VI.75–83 is the basis for all of this bit.
24. Plutarch, Sayings of the Spartans, 223B.
25. When later on trial for not continuing the campaign Cleomenes claimed that when he had entered the temple to ask Hera if he would be successful in taking the town of Argos itself, a sheet of fire had flashed out from the breast of the statue of Hera, which he had interpreted as a sign that his campaign had accomplished all the goddess intended to let him. This was accepted by the Spartan authorities as 'a credible and reasonable defence' and he was fully acquitted. Herodotus, VI.82.
26. Thucydides, *The Peloponnesian War*, V.54–55.
27. Herodotus, *The Histories*, IX.26–70.
28. Plutarch, *Aemilius Paulus*, 17–19.
29. Xenophon, *Hellenika*, IV.7.
30. The campaign and incident are excellently narrated in Philip Matyszak, *Mithridates the Great: Rome's Indomitable Enemy* (Barnsley, 2008), pp. 105–6, but here I have preferred the translation given in Bill Thayer's translation, available online at http://penelope.uchicago.edu/Thayer/E/Roman/Texts/Plutarch/Lives/Lucullus*.html
31. Eusebius, *Vita Constantini*, I.28.2 quoted by Elizabeth James in *Constantine the Great General* (Barnsley, 2012).
32. *Ibid*, I.29.

Chapter 8: An Army Marches on its Stomach (and its Liver)

33. Frontinus, *Stratagems*, II.v.12.
34. Frontinus, *Stratagems*, II.v.13 (Hannibal) and II.v.14 (Gracchus).
35. T.E. Lawrence, *Seven Pillars of Wisdom* (London, 1935) pp. 131–2.

Chapter 9: Unlikely Survivors

36. Quintus Curtius Rufus, *The History of Alexander*, IX.13, translated by John Yardley with note by Waldemaar Heckel (London, 1984), p. 223.
37. The primary source for both incidents is Procopius but they can be found in Ian Hughes' excellent *Belisarius* (Barnsley, 2009), p. 151
38. James Arnold, *Crisis in the Snows* (Lexington, 2007), p. 305.

Chapter 10: Siege the Day

39. Polybius, *The Histories*, V, 97, translation from the marvellous www.Lacuscurtius.com
40. Herodotus, *The Histories*, I.84–5.
41. The incident is related in the old Norse chronicle, *Heimskringla* but I am indebted to Nic Fields (author of many fine books on ancient warfare) for this one. Thanks Nic.
42. Tacitus, *Annals of Imperial Rome*, XIV.
43. Frontinus, *Stratagems*, II.ix.5.
44. Frontinus, *Stratagems*, III.7.6.
45. The chain is mentioned in Frontinus, *Stratagems*, III.xiv.2 but Livy provides the main narrative here: Livy, *History of Rome*, XXIII.19.
46. 'Bravo', *Time Magazine*, 25 July 1949.
47. Richard Holmes, *The Western Front* (London, p. 100–1).

Chapter 11: Stranger Things Happen at Sea

48. This quote from Hawker's biography of Carew is, like most of this entry, taken from the excellent account by Stuart Vine on the official Mary Rose website: www.maryrose.org
49. David Hepper, *British Warship Losses in the Ironclad Era 1860–1919* (London, 2006), p. 20.
50. Hepper, *British Warship Losses*, p. 95.
51. http://en.wikipedia.org/wiki/USS_Tang_(SS-306), which cites Richard H. O'Kane's own account, *Clear the Bridge!* (Chicago, 1977).
52. Jak Malmann Showell, *The U-boat Century* (London, 2006), p. 81.
53. Cornelius Nepos, *Lives of Emminent Commanders*, XXIII, translated by Rev. John Selby Watson, 1886.
54. Showell, *The U-boat Century*, pp. 33 and 81.
55. BBC News Online, 8 March 2000.

Chapter 12: What Do You Want – A Medal?

56. Roy Ingleton, *Kent VCs* (Barnsley, 2011), pp. 4–5.
57. Ingleton, *Kent VCs*, pp. 28–9.
58. Sir Richard Holmes, *Sahib: The British Soldier in India* (London, 2005), p. 314.
59. http://en.wikipedia.org/wiki/HMS_Glowworm_(H92).
60. http://en.wikipedia.org/wiki/Lloyd_Allan_Trigg; also www.victoriacross.org.uk, citing *London Gazette*, 2 November 1943.

Notes

61. John Duncan and John Walton, *Heroes for Victoria* (Spellmount, Staplehurst, 1991), p. 24.
62. Sir Richard Holmes, *Sahib*, p. 506.
63. Duncan and Walton, *Heroes for Victoria*, p. 22.

Chapter 13: Undiplomatic Responses

64. Plutarch, *Sayings of the Spartans*, 233 E – from Bill Thayer's excellent Lacus Curtius website.
65. David Chandler, *The Art of Warfare in the Age of Marlborough* (Spellmount, Staplehurst, 1990), p. 246.

Chapter 15: Miscellaneous

66. Herodotus, *The Histories*, I.82.
67. Philip J. Haythornthwaite, *Napoleonic Cavalry* (London, 2001), p. 107.
68. Andrew Nagorski, *The Greatest Battle: The Fight for Moscow 1941–2* (London, 2008), p. 197.

Chapter 16: Weird and Wonderful Weapons

69. Xenophon, *Anabasis*, I.8, translated by Rex Warner and published in the Penguin Classics series as *The Persian Expedition* (London, 1972), p. 88–9.
70. Arrian, *Anabsis Alexandri* iii.13, translated by Aubrey de Sélincourt and published in the Penguin Classics series as *The Campaigns of Alexander* (London, 1971), p. 168.
71. Ralph D. Sawyer, *Fire and Water: The Art of Incendiary and Aquatic Warfare in China* (Boulder, Colorado, 2004), p. 120. A televised modern reconstruction proved the method of firing the crossbows was viable: *Ancient Discoveries* is repeated fairly regularly on History Channel.
72. Steven J. Zaloga et al., *Soviet Tanks in Combat 1941–45* (Hong Kong, 1997), p. 72.

Index

Index

Boston Dynamics, 150
Boudicca (Boadicea), 129
Bourdesoule, French general, 124
boy soldiers in British army, 112
Brandywine Creek, Battle of (1777)
Brigte, Máel (the Bucktoothed), 25–6
Briscoe Station, Battle of (1863)
Britain, British, 9–10, 31, 34–5, 41, 60, 62, 69–71, 108–12
Bruizer, HMS, 98
Brummbär (Grizzly Bear), tank, 30
buffaloes, as anti-elephant obstacle, 19

Caesar, Julius, 9–10, 12, 129,
Calvo, Count, 119
Cambyses, Persian king, 21,
camels: disguised as elephants, 13–15, 16; smoking, 20; as living flasks, 60–1
Canada, Canadians, 130, 135
Canute, Danish king, 28
Carew, Vice Admiral Sir George, 95–6
Carthage, Carthaginians, 7, 32–3, 52, 59, 86, 104
Casilinum, Siege of (216 BC), 86–7
cats, in incendiary attacks, 81
cat-scrapper (Katzbalger), 29
Cassivellaunus, ancient British leader, 10
Chaeronea, Battle of (86 BC), 128
Chandragupta Maurya, 5, 81
Charge of the Light Brigade, 27
Charles VI of France, 122
chariots: elephant-drawn, 2; scythed, 126–9; unmanned, 129–30
Chasseurs à Cheval, 71
Chatak, horse disguised as elephant, 15–16
chickens, sacred, 51–2
China, Chinese, 20, 32, 37, 42, 129
Christie, ensign of 44th Foot, 70–1
Chromios, Argive warrior, 123
Churchill Crocodile, tank, 31
Churchill, Sir Winston, 134

Cleomenes I of Sparta, 45–7, 120
Cleopatra VII, 6
Clisthenes of Sicyon, 85
Constantine I (the Great), Roman Emperor, 55–7
Cooke, John R, Union general, 43
Corbulo, Gnaeus Domitius, Roman general, 83
cow sinks Japanese boat, 103
Crab (Sherman Crab) tank, 31
Cranbonne, General, 119
Crimean War, 27, 108,
Croesus of Lydia, 44–5, 79–80
Cunaxa, Battle of (401 BC), 127–8
Curtiss Sparrowhawk, 142
Cyclone bio-fuel engines, 152
Cyrus the Great, Persian king, 79–80
Cyrus the Younger, Persian prince, 127
Crusades, 23–4; Seventh Crusade, 24
Cutilas, Roman guardsman, 68
Cynoscephelae, Battle of (197 BC), 16

Damietta, Battle of (1249), 24
Darius I, Persian king, 113
Darius III, Persian king, 127
DARPA (Defence Advanced Research Projects Agency), 152
D'Autreche, Gautier, 23–4
da Vinci, Leonardo, 129
Derouft, Jules, balloonist, 92
Dettingen, Battle of (1743), 34
devotio, ritual self-sacrifice, 52–4
Dingo, armoured car, 31
Dio, Roman historian, 16
Diodorus Siculus, Greek historian, 3, 13–14
Dionysius of Halicarnassus, Greek Historian, 18
Directorate of Miscellaneous Weapons Development (DMWD), 132
dogs, incendiary, 81; Soviet anti-tank, 138–9; US demolition, 139

159

Index

Index

Enjoyed reading this book?

Want to read more wonderfully wacky
true to life stories?

Then read on to discover
the opening chapters from
Fool Britannia by Sue Blackhall,
a book full of headline making
newspaper stories from the past year
that beggar belief...

1

Aisle Be Blowed

When Krys Gunton decided to pop into her local Tesco store after a morning's riding, the one thing she did not expect was to be saddled with the insult of being called 'smelly'. Neither did she expect to be asked to leave the shop, Tesco Metro in Romford, Essex.

Miss Gunton had walked into the shop wearing jodhpurs and boots, having just finished an enjoyable hour on her horse Monty. But she was confronted by a security guard who asked her to leave on the grounds of health and safety because she apparently 'smelled too much'. Said Miss Gunton: 'At first I didn't understand him. But then it became clear that someone else in the shop complained about the smell to him. He kept repeating "You're smelling too much." I asked him what he thought I should do about it and he suggested I should change my clothes. I just told him that I didn't have any spare clothes and that there was nowhere to change anyway. The whole situation was completely ridiculous.'

A spokesman for Tesco said of the incident in January 2009: 'We apologise for any confusion or upset caused but we did ask the customer to leave for health and safety reasons. The customer was asked politely to leave the store as she had manure on her riding boots which is of course not acceptable in a store which sells food.' Miss Gunton, a 29-year-old university administrator, was adamant that there was no horse muck on her – only mud – and added: 'Before I went in I made sure I wasn't trailing mess everywhere. It was not like I was covered in

7

horse muck. It was just "eau de horse!" I was totally humiliated in front of a shop full of people and felt forced to dump my shopping and simply walk out of there.'

Tesco hit the news again that month when 49-year-old Maurice Harris was forced to prove he was over 18 before the shop in Bedworth, Warwickshire would sell him a bag of party poppers. And in Tesco's in Chelmsford, a 23-year-old policeman was refused a bottle of wine because his partner with him was only 18. At yet another Tesco store, this time in Flitwick, Bedfordshire, a 48-year-old woman was asked to prove she was over 18 before she could buy a T-shirt bearing a Guinness logo. Oh, and good old Tesco hit the headlines in February when a 9-year-old girl with learning difficulties was banned from carrying a helium balloon into its superstore on the Tower Park leisure complex in Poole, Dorset. Little Alex Pearson had been given the balloon after enjoying a meal at the nearby Chiquito Mexican restaurant. Her mum, 44-year-old Marion Pearson, tied the balloon to Alex's wrist so it would not blow away before they entered the Tesco shop. But they were stopped by a security guard who said it was a health and safety risk. Said Mrs Pearson: 'Alex didn't understand why she wasn't allowed in and I told the security guard to explain it to her. He couldn't even look her in the eye. I think he was too embarrassed.' A Tesco spokesman said that on that day a number of children had come into the store and let the balloons loose either accidentally or deliberately. 'Unfortunately they were getting trapped on the ceiling and blocking the sprinkler system and they are pretty difficult to retrieve. The managers decided to use their discretion.' In November a group of students, all over 18, went to the Tesco store in Warwick to buy a bottle of wine, a birthday cake and a packet of candles. They were asked for ID, which six could produce but one couldn't. So the cashier refused to sell them the wine. They said they would just take the cake and the candles then. Sorry, said the cashier, but you can't have the candles, either. Why not? No ID. The students were left with just the cake.

Standing 6 feet tall and aged 20, Stephen Stuart never experienced any problems over looking his age – except when he tried to buy a 12A-rated DVD from his local Sainsbury store in Didcot, Oxfordshire, in October. Despite sporting stubble and looking anything but a lad less than 12 years old, Stephen was nevertheless refused his purchase of the *X-Men Origins: Wolverine* DVD when he could not produce any ID. Said Stephen: 'I asked the girl at the till: "Do I look 11 or under?" The last thing I thought I would need to buy a 12A DVD at my age and height was ID. If I was buying a bottle of whisky or an X-rated film I'd understand. But this was a DVD about a comic superhero. I get served in pubs and clubs without a glance . . .' After the cashier and a supervisor both refused to sell Stephen the £9.99 DVD, his 53-year-old dad Ian took over the transaction – after cheekily showing his driving licence. 'She told me not to be so silly,' said Ian. A spokesman for Sainsbury's commented: 'Customers who look under 25 are asked for ID on age-related items and that includes all DVDs.' A similar incident happened at the Marks & Spencer store in South Mimms when Andree Evans bought a birthday card and the till automatically sounded the 'check they are over 25' alarm because the card had a picture of bottles of wine, wine glasses and a corkscrew.

Still in the silly department of over-the-counter craziness, 15-year-old Jaz Bhogal was banned from buying a bag of wine gums at a discount store in Wisbech, Cambridgeshire because he needed to be 18-plus to buy anything containing alcohol. Jaz was even chased down the street with his purchase, ordered to return to the 99p Store and had his sweets confiscated. He was, however, refunded his 99p. Said Jaz: 'I couldn't believe it. I was asked how old I was and when I said I was 15, I was told they couldn't sell me the sweets. They said they had wine in them and pointed to the word "wine" on the packet. I was absolutely speechless.' Added mum Sue, 36: 'I thought Jaz was joking when he came home and told me what had happened. It is ridiculous and I would have been really cross if I had asked him to buy them for me.' Wine gums, of course, do not contain wine. A spokesman for 99p Stores admitted: 'Because the Wisbech store opened fairly recently there seems to have been an unfortunate glitch. We have rectified this and are sure it will not happen again at any of our UK stores.' He added: 'To show that we have a good sense of humour we would like to offer Jaz a nine-item voucher in the store – on condition that at least one of those products is wine gums . . .'

When 70-year-old retired oil worker Chris Pether tried to buy two lemons at the self-service checkout at the Asda store in Aberdeen, he was greeted with a message telling him he had bought too many. Obviously a little taken aback by this, Mr Pether sought the assistance of a shop supervisor who told him that because teenagers tended to throw fruit at people, health and safety rules now prevented them from selling more than one loose lemon, orange or grapefruit. Even more bizarre, the pensioner was told he could buy a bag of ten lemons because they weren't 'loose' and were smaller, meaning their potential as a lethal weapon was lessened. He didn't take up the offer, instead choosing to turn his lemon purchase into two separate transactions and thereby getting round the rules. Said Mr Pether: 'It takes some believing. It was so ludicrous but it's part and parcel of the expansion of the nanny state.' Commented a spokesman for Asda: 'It sounds like one of our colleagues was having a really bad day. People can buy as many lemons, oranges and grapefruits as they like.'

Despite her protests, management consultant Jackie Slater was not allowed to purchase two bottles of wine because she was in the company of her 17-year-old daughter and 18-year-old niece – who the staff at the Morrison's store in Leeds thought Mrs Slater might be buying the alcohol for. She was asked to show some ID and was quizzed by an assistant about the two young girls chatting at the end of the checkout. Said Mrs Slater: 'I told her I was really flattered, but I was the wrong side of 50 . . . the assistant asked "Are they with you?" I said they'd come to help me carry the bags back to the car. The assistant said: "You could be buying the wine for them. It's the policy – I have to see everyone's ID to make sure they are all over 18." I was embarrassed, there was a huge queue building up and my daughter found it all excruciating,' said Mrs Slater, who describes the incident as 'the silliest bit of jobsworth nonsense' she had ever come across. 'It comes to something when a mother can't take her daughter shopping without being made to feel like a criminal.' In vain, Mrs Slater insisted that the wine was for herself and her husband, Peter. But the assistant and then the store manager refused to budge. Morrison's head office backed the store with a spokesman saying: 'Under current licensing laws, stores are unable to sell an alcoholic product to a customer they believe could be buying for a minor or for someone who is unable to prove their age. We take our responsibility with regard to selling alcohol very seriously. The rules are in place to protect our customers and their families, as well as local communities who, in the majority of cases, appreciate our vigilance in the sale of age-restricted products.' But the company did not contest Mrs Slater's version of events. The assistant even agreed that she would have sold the wine to a mother who had younger children with her because 'no one would buy wine for a 12-year-old'.

A misunderstanding over a mum's support of British troops injured while fighting in Afghanistan led to her being refused service at an Asda store in Rochdale. Beth Hoyle was wearing a Help for Heroes wristband which was sadly interpreted by an Asian cashier as the mother of three supporting war in both Afghanistan and Iraq. He was backed up by a store supervisor who told Beth the cashier was entitled to his point of view and to refuse to serve her 'because of what she was wearing'. Said Beth: 'I told him it was nothing to do with the war, but about supporting injured troops. I complained to a supervisor, but he said it was his right not to serve me. I was disgusted.' A spokesman for Asda said they were 'shocked' by the claim but could not find any evidence of the incident taking place, adding that the supermarket chain was a supporter of Help for Heroes and sold its campaign wristbands and badges.

In a separate incident, staff at the Asda store on Hayling Island, Hampshire, asked 61-year-old Ed Spencer to verify he was over 18 before he was allowed to buy a can of non-alcoholic shandy.

It seemed the obvious thing to do . . . Sue Savage, a little on the short side and in an ankle brace after breaking her leg, asked her much taller daughter Tara to stretch up to pick vodka and rum mixers from a high shelf at their local Co-op store in Cranbrook, Kent. But when she tried to pay, Mrs Savage was accused of trying to supply alcohol to a minor. Already a bit stressed over the cocktail party she was planning, she tried to explain why she was buying the drink. But a supervisor insisted she leave the bottles of booze in the shop. The mother-of-two later returned on her own to have another go but was told again – this time by the shop manager – that it was believed she was buying drink for a minor. Thoroughly frustrated now, Mrs Savage threw a £10 note on the counter and left with her purchases, with the warning she was breaking the law ringing in her ears. Now in a complete dither, she called the police for advice. They arrived two hours later, advised her to return the drink, arrested her and gave her an £80 fixed penalty notice. Determined to take the matter further, she stormed: 'It's ridiculous. Does this mean anyone with children cannot go shopping with them and buy alcohol?' A spokesman for the Co-op said: 'We are a respectable retailer and have a legal responsibility to ensure that alcohol is not sold to children.'

Queries over customers' age when buying an item with even a slight relation to alcohol or when some other loony PC bit of legislation comes into play is commonplace nowadays. But even then, it was hard to work out why 24-year-old office worker Christine Cuddihy had a Tesco checkout cashier quibbling over a 51p slice of quiche – because Christine 'looked under 21'. The bizarre shopping experience happened at the Tesco store in Cannons Park, Coventry, in January 2010 when Christine, from nearby Leamington Spa, popped in to buy the quiche for her supper. Tesco, as we already know, have a rather strange approach to customer relations sometimes. On this occasion the cashier told Christine that she could not go through the checkout with her quiche because of the doubts about her age, saying: 'You don't look over 21. I need some proof of age.' Christine obviously queried this and was met with the response: 'We have to be really strict now and this applies to quiche bought over the counter.' There was something of a heated debate between the two women, but eager to avoid further embarrassment with a queue growing longer behind her, Christine produced her driving licence and fled. She naturally had much to say about the surreal encounter. 'It was very embarrassing. What on earth is dangerous about a slice of quiche? There was nothing suspicious about me and it's not even like I was buying a whole quiche to binge on. It was rush-hour and the shop was really busy. I was so insulted that they thought I couldn't be trusted with a harmless snack. I was really embarrassed and just wanted to get out of the shop. The irony of the whole thing is that I've bought alcohol from there dozens of times without being asked for ID. I've racked my brains to come up with an explanation but I can't find one. The whole thing is ridiculous.' Tesco later apologised and admitted shoppers did not have to prove their age when they bought quiche. Confessed a spokesman: 'We're at a loss to say what happened here. We couldn't find the staff member who asked for the ID. Age-related prompts at till are set centrally and there obviously isn't one on quiche.'

. . . But is there a Tesco policy of treating all teenagers as prospective thieves? The question had to be asked when in February it was revealed that staff at the Tesco Express store in Halesowen in the West Midlands were ordering school-children to remove their blazers and deposit their bags at a checkpoint before they were allowed in to buy snacks. One witness was horrified, saying: 'I feel it is inappropriate for an adult to ask teenage boys and girls to remove clothing and trust them with their possessions, especially as all teenagers and schoolchildren were being branded thieves. When confronted, a senior member of staff at the store replied: "Don't tell me. I'm just the manager."' One feels the schoolchildren could have got their own back by pointing out the spelling mistakes in a sign warning about the new policy: 'Due to issues anybody in school uniform will be asked to leave there jacket/blazer and bags by the front door unless accomipant with an adult.' Defending the policy a Tesco spokesman said: 'We take our responsibilities seriously. We've had a number of issues in this store and complaints from other customers. We have discussed this with the local school and have regretfully had to restrict the number of schoolchildren coming into the store.' Founder of the lobby group Parents Outloud, Margaret Morrisey, did not accept this explanation, saying: 'It is a horrible policy, effectively saying that all the children are thieves. It would be far better to have staff keep a close eye on them, or limit the number of pupils allowed in at once. If there is a problem, surely it would have been better for the managers to talk to the school and have it dealt with. You can't get young people to take clothes off to enter a shop. It is just not right.'

To read more stories from *Fool Britannia*
or to read one of our fantastic
new fiction titles overleaf you can
order your copies direct from
PEN & SWORD BOOKS

Please call 01226 734222

Or order online via our website:
www.pen-and-sword.co.uk

9781781590713 •
368 pages • £7.99

A brutally honest portrayal of the realities of war, this novel relays the story of fifteen-year-old Thomas Elkin as he engages in the First World War. A tale of conflict, both global and personal, and of redemption, this is a novel that has the potential to rank alongside the best of retrospective First World War literature. Accepting the blame for the accidental death of his recently conscripted brother, Elkin switches identity with his dead sibling and enters into the fray of the conflict. His burning ambition is to die a glorious death in his brother's name.

Believing that in fully submitting to the reality of war he is atoning for his sins, he faces all the attendant horrors with a steel will and a poignant resignation.

His personal conflict sees itself mirrored in the wider events and soon the two are inextricably linked raising issues of mortality, morality, guilt and faith. This novel enacts the kind of existential crises experienced on the battlefield with the constant threat of the imminent and fatal danger a companion.

Written with deft skill and sensitivity for the subject matter at hand, this is a piece of stylish work that places the reader at the heart of the action. Featuring nuanced characters and vivid action scenes, it works to evoke a real sense of the times as the story unfolds.

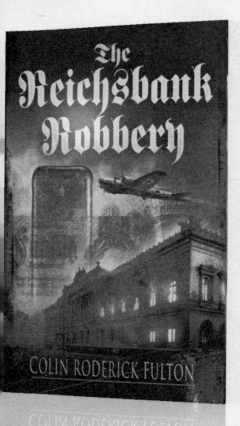

9781781590782 •
336 pages • £8.99

In February 1945 the US Air Force launched the largest day time bombing offensive against Berlin, dropping over 2,250 tons of bombs on the German capital.

The Reichsbank, Germany's state bank, received 21 direct hits. This left the building badly damaged, its vaults unsafe and meant that most of its contents were at risk.

The German authorities made the decision to take most of the Reichsbank's treasure away and hide it for safekeeping. Some $200 million US in gold bars, weighing around 100 tons, plus much of the paper currency reserves, as well as a great deal of foreign currency (approximately $4 million in US currency alone) was sent in trains from Berlin.

All this loot was placed in a salt mine at a place called Merkers. This was captured intact by the US Army. After this disaster, the Germans spent the next six weeks transferring their remaining bullion and currency reserves around what remained of the Reich in armoured trains, an area that included parts of northern Italy, Czechoslovakia, Austria and Germany, looking for somewhere safe.

Much of the treasure actually either ended up back in Berlin, was stolen, disappeared or, was captured, mainly by American troops and the SS.

This novel, by Colin Roderick Fulton, imagines one plot which could have been enacted around this time. The mystery surrounding the locations and ultimate destiny of the liberated treasures provides fertile ground on which to impose such a fiction. Secrecy, intrigue, and fast paced action combine to create a well paced novel, sure to appeal to fans of wartime fiction.

9781781590843 •
208 pages • £8.99

This enthralling piece of work by first-time novelist Robert Southworth explores the avenue history could have run down if Spartacus had survived the slave rebellion in 73BC, an uprising whose aftermath didn't deliver the remains of the famous slave leader. The brute force of this famous figure of Roman history is relayed, and the events of the period re-imagined to great effect. The work is sure to appeal to fans of Roman history, as well as those enamored by stories of action and adventure. Whilst the figure of Spartacus continues to hold massive appeal for contemporary audiences, this work offers a fresh vision of the Roman era; a dark and brutal reenactment of high gladiatorial drama.

9781781590645 •
320 pages • £9.99

It is 1861. Tom Wells is in pursuit of a girl from North Carolina. He accepts an offer from his employer to leave the quiet obscurity of his job as an office boy in a London shipping firm to cross the Atlantic to Nassau in the Bahamas. Now he must face the hazards of the Union blockade of the Confederate ports in the American Civil War. Tom's bravado may help him with the dangers of running the blockade, but how will he cope with the conflicting issues of love, loyalty and morality as he becomes entangled with a lady of easy virtue in Nassau?

Tom's adventures take him through the perilous triangle between Nassau, Charleston and Wilmington NC, where he must smuggle arms and munitions through a gauntlet of Union warships to the Southern ports, bringing cotton and tobacco back to Nassau.

David Kent-Lemon presents us here with a fast paced and dynamic narrative, exploring a fascinating, dramatic and less well known corner of that extraordinary conflict – the American Civil War. The characters are finely drawn, with the balance between deceit and morality offset by courage and humour. The realism and historical accuracy of the background complete the picture.

As the Civil War reaches its climax, so does the drama in Tom's life, heightened by the historical events within which he is embroiled.

9781781590683 •
496 pages • £9.99

Set in a period of great social unrest, this novel explores the various rivalries acted out between Royalist and Parliamentarian factions in 17th Century Britain.

The real-life historical figure of Elizabeth Murray serves as the novels central protagonist; Countess Dysart and Duchess of Lauderdale, she inhabited Ham House, a Jacobean mansion built on the River Thames at Petersham. Throughout the reigns of Charles I, Charles II, James II, William and Mary, she became deeply embroiled in the politics of the Civil War. Wielding a great deal of influence due to her elevated position, and partaking in her fair share of adventure, she found herself right at the heart of the action. It is into this which we are thrust, as Anita Seymour takes us on a breathtaking ride through the landscape of a divided England.

9781781592403 •
320 pages • £9.99

When Germany's leading tank ace meets the Steppe Fox it's a fight to the death. Faced with overwhelming odds Kampfgruppe von Schroif needs a better tank and fast; but the new Tiger tank is still on the drawing board and von Schroif must overcome bureaucracy, espionage and relentless Allied bombing to get the Tiger into battle in time to meet the ultimate challenge.

Based on a true story of combat on the Russian Front, this powerful new novel is written by Emmy™ Award winning writer Bob Carruthers and newcomer Sinclair McLay. It tells the gripping saga of how the Tiger tank was born and a legend was forged in the heat of combat. Gritty, intense and breath-taking in its detail, this sprawling epic captures the reality of the lives and deaths of the tank crews fighting for survival on the Eastern Front, a remarkable novel worthy of comparison with 'Das Boot'.

9781781591000 •
272 pages • £9.99

When two of the nuns creating the Bayeux Tapestry fall from the tower of the Priory of St Thomas the Apostle, Abbess Eleanor and her protégé, Therese, are sent to investigate. As the adventures unfold, the intrigue created between the Norman Princes and Bishops, as well as the tensions between the conquerors and the native Britons, deepen to great and dramatic effect. Mary Bale has captured the spirit and feel of the times which she evokes in this, her first novel. The sense of intrigue is heightened by the writing style which is taut, fast-paced, and heavy with a sense of mystery. This extensively researched novel is sure to appeal to those looking for an evocative tale of adventure and intrigue, made vivid by fascinating period details.

9781781591734 •
256 pages • £9.99

Peenemünde: windswept corner of the Third Reich and birthplace of the space age. Otto Fischer, a severely wounded Luftwaffe officer and former criminal investigator, is summoned to solve a seemingly incomprehensible case: the murder of a leading rocket engineer during a devastating air-raid. With only days until the SS assume control of the production of a remarkable new weapon, Fischer must find a motive and perpetrator from among several thousand scientists, technicians, soldiers and forced labourers. As he struggles to get the measure of a secretive, brilliant world in which imagination moves far beyond the limits of technology, what at first appears to be a solitary crime draws him into a labyrinth of conspiracy, betrayal and treason.

McDermott brings skills previously honed whilst producing well-researched history books to the discipline of writing fiction, creating work that is both historically accurate and evocative as well as stylish in a literary sense.

THE
TRIANGLE
TRADE

GEOFF WOODLAND

9781781591741 •
272 pages • £9.99

In 1804, Liverpool was the largest slave trading port in Great Britain, yet her influential traders felt threatened by the success, in Parliament, of the anti-slavery movement. Few, in Liverpool, condemned the 'Trade'. William King, son of a Liverpool slave trader, sickened by what he experienced aboard a Spanish slaver, was one of the few who did speak out. This epic, set during the dying days of this despicable practice, weaves themes of generational change, moral wickedness, greed, romance, and the fortunes of war as they impact upon the lives of a father and son caught up in the turmoil that preceded the implementation of the British Trade Act of 1807, which would end Britain's involvement in the slave trade.

The city of Liverpool is one still scarred by its past involvement with the morally contemptible Triangle Trade. Indeed, the cities prosperity was built on the profits of slavery, and the reverberations of this inheritance continue to impact on the city today. This novel roots the reader firmly in a city on the brink of change, evoking a real sense of the struggles at play, and informing our understanding of the realities of slavery, those who fueled its continuation and those who brought about its eventual cessation, as well as the legacy inherited by the City of Liverpool and the wider world.